MOUTHWATERING
MAIN COURSES

◆

Reader's Digest Healthy Cooking Library

MOUTHWATERING MAIN COURSES

Published by The Reader's Digest Association Limited

LONDON ◆ NEW YORK ◆ SYDNEY ◆ CAPE TOWN ◆ MONTREAL

The Reader's Digest Healthy Cooking Library was edited and
designed by The Reader's Digest Association Ltd, London.
These recipes and illustrations have previously appeared in
GREAT RECIPES FOR GOOD HEALTH, published in 1993
by Reader's Digest, UK.

First Edition

Copyright © 1995
The Reader's Digest Association Limited,
Berkeley Square House,
Berkeley Square,
London W1X 6AB.
Copyright © 1995
Reader's Digest Association Far East Limited.
Philippines Copyright © 1995
Reader's Digest Association Far East Limited.

Printed in Italy

ISBN 0 276 42176 0

Consultant Editor Pat Alburey
Nutritional Consultant Editor Cynthia Robinson, BSc
Nutritional Consultant Moya de Wet, BSc, SRD

Recipes created by Pat Alburey, Valerie Barrett, Jackie Burrow,
Carole Handslip, Petra Jackson, Meg Jansz, Angela Kingsbury,
Danielle Nay, Louise Pickford, Jane Suthering, Judith Taylor,
Hilaire Walden

CONTENTS

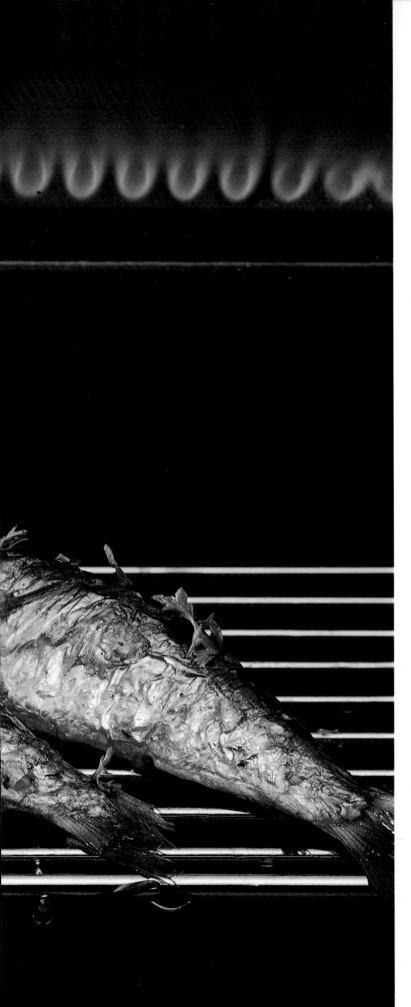

FISH AND SHELLFISH

Quick to cook and easy to digest, fish offers the benefits of animal protein without the overload of saturated fat. The range is wide, from meaty halibut to rich pink salmon, delicate sole to melting mackerel, with prawns and shellfish extending the choice. Sizzling from the grill, chilled in a wine jelly or baked in a paper parcel, they can make healthy family meals and grander dishes for guests.

Sea bream and vegetable parcels

ONE SERVING

CALORIES 180

TOTAL FAT 5g

SATURATED FAT 1g

CARBOHYDRATES 3g

ADDED SUGAR 0

FIBRE 2g

SODIUM 195mg

The paper wrapping seals in the moisture and taste of the bream, while the vegetables remain firm. Rice mixed with lemon zest and chopped fennel makes a subtle accompaniment.

SERVES 4
PREPARATION TIME: 15 minutes
COOKING TIME: 20 minutes
OVEN: Preheat to 200°C (400°F, gas mark 6)

1½ tablespoons olive oil
2 spring onions, trimmed and chopped
1 tablespoon lemon juice
¼ level teaspoon paprika
1 large carrot, peeled and cut into strips
1 large leek, trimmed, cut into strips and washed
2oz (60g) mushrooms, wiped and sliced
2 bream, each about 1lb (450g), scaled
and cleaned
Freshly ground black pepper
10 slices lemon

1 Mix 1 tablespoon of the oil with the spring onions, lemon juice and paprika.

2 Blanch the carrot, leek and mushrooms in boiling water for 1 minute, then drain well.

3 Cut 2 sheets of nonstick baking paper large enough to wrap round the fish, and brush with the remaining oil. Place a fish in the centre of each sheet and scatter with the carrot, leek and mushrooms. Trickle half the oil mixture over each fish, season with pepper and lay the lemon slices along the top. Fold the paper sheets closely round the fish and tuck under securely at the ends.

4 Put the parcels on a baking tray and cook in the heated oven for 20 minutes, then open them and see if the fish flakes easily. If necessary, return the parcels to the oven for a further 5 minutes. Lift the parcels onto large, warmed serving dishes to take to the table.

> **TIP**
> *To divide each fish, run a sharp knife horizontally along the backbone to free the flesh above the bones. Lift off the top fillet carefully and serve. Remove the bones from the remaining fillet and serve.*

Steamed cod with ginger

ONE SERVING

CALORIES 195

TOTAL FAT 7g

SATURATED FAT 1g

CARBOHYDRATES 4g

ADDED SUGAR 0

FIBRE 2g

SODIUM 130mg

SERVES 4
PREPARATION TIME: 10 minutes
COOKING TIME: 15 minutes

1 leek, trimmed, quartered lengthways, washed and
thickly sliced
3 green sticks celery, trimmed and thinly sliced
1 medium red onion, peeled, thinly sliced and
separated into rings

1 large carrot, peeled and thinly sliced
4 level teaspoons peeled and grated root ginger
4 cod steaks, each about 6oz (175g)
6 allspice berries, coarsely ground or crushed
2 spring onions, trimmed and thinly sliced
2 large sprigs parsley
Sprigs of fresh oregano or thyme
2 tablespoons lemon juice
2 tablespoons olive oil

1 Pour 1in (25mm) of water into the bottom of a fish-steamer or into a large saucepan with a bamboo steamer set on it. Bring the water to the boil. Mix the leek, celery, red onion, carrot and ginger and spread in an even layer on the steaming rack. Cover and steam for 5 minutes.

2 Arrange the cod steaks on the vegetables and sprinkle evenly with the allspice and spring onions. Lay the parsley and oregano or thyme on top, cover and steam for 5-6 minutes, or until the fish becomes opaque and the flesh flakes easily when tested with a fork.

3 Carefully lift the cod steaks onto a warmed serving dish and spoon the crisp vegetables round them, discarding the herbs. Cover the dish and keep hot.

4 Remove the rack or bamboo steamer from the pan. Pour the liquid into a small saucepan and boil it rapidly to reduce it to about half a cupful. Whisk in the lemon juice and oil and pour the sauce over the fish and vegetables.

Serve the cod steaks with new potatoes tossed in a little chopped parsley.

There is the simplicity and aroma of Chinese cuisine in these cod steaks steamed with vegetables and herbs and sharpened by the fire of ginger.

Haddock and goat's cheese soufflé

ONE SERVING	
CALORIES	235
TOTAL FAT	12g
SATURATED FAT	4g
CARBOHYDRATES	13g
ADDED SUGAR	0
FIBRE	0
SODIUM	715mg

TIP
To give the soufflé a good rise, do not beat the egg whites to a dry foam. Slightly softer foam expands more during cooking.

SERVES 4
PREPARATION TIME: 30 minutes
COOKING TIME: 35 minutes
OVEN: Preheat to 190°C (375°F, gas mark 5)

8oz (225g) smoked haddock, skinned, boned, washed and cut into small pieces
8fl oz (225ml) skimmed milk
1oz (30g) polyunsaturated margarine
4 level tablespoons plain flour
2 eggs, separated, plus 2 egg whites, size 2
2oz (60g) medium-fat soft goat's cheese
Freshly ground black pepper

1 Simmer the haddock in 4 tablespoons of the milk in a covered saucepan for 2-3 minutes, until it will just flake. Drain the liquid into the rest of the milk.

2 Melt the margarine in a saucepan, stir in the flour and cook for 1-2 minutes. Gradually stir in the milk and bring the sauce to the boil, stirring continuously. Reduce the heat and simmer for 2-3 minutes, stirring frequently, until the sauce is thick. Remove from the heat and whisk in the egg yolks.

3 Mix the haddock and cheese in a large bowl and season lightly with pepper. Pour in the sauce and mix in gently.

4 Lightly grease a deep soufflé dish 7¼ in (19cm) in diameter. Whisk the egg whites until they will hold soft peaks. Fold one-quarter of the egg white into the fish sauce, using a metal spoon, to lighten the mixture. Then carefully fold in the remaining egg white. Pour into the prepared soufflé dish and cook in the heated oven for about 35 minutes, or until well risen and golden brown, but creamy in the centre.

Robust as a mature hard cheese in its flavour, the soft goat's cheese marries well with the strong taste of the smoked fish in this soufflé.

Grilled halibut with red pepper sauce

ONE SERVING	
CALORIES 135	
TOTAL FAT 4g	
SATURATED FAT 1g	
CARBOHYDRATES 2g	
ADDED SUGAR 0	
FIBRE 1g	
SODIUM 105mg	

SERVES 4
PREPARATION TIME: 10 minutes
COOKING TIME: 15 minutes

2 medium red peppers
2 cloves garlic, unpeeled
2 teaspoons red wine vinegar
1 teaspoon olive oil
4 halibut steaks, each about 5oz (150g)
Freshly ground black pepper
Sprigs of flat-leaf parsley to garnish

Aubergine wedges, sautéed in a little olive oil, and french bread go well with the fish, while a crisp mixed salad adds a light touch. For a special occasion, you could serve asparagus baked in white wine, and new potatoes tossed in finely chopped chives.

1 Grill the peppers under a moderate heat for 5-8 minutes, turning occasionally until the skins turn brown and start to blister. Put the peppers in a small bowl and cover with a clean, damp cloth to keep in the steam and loosen the skins.

2 Meanwhile, wrap the cloves of garlic in a piece of foil, and grill for 5 minutes to soften. Leave to cool, then peel the cloves and set aside.

3 When the peppers are cool enough to handle, skin them and remove the seeds and stalks, working over a bowl to catch the juice. Blend the peppers, their juice, the garlic, vinegar and oil to a purée, using a food processor or a food mill.

4 Line the grill pan with foil. Lightly oil the grill rack, arrange the halibut steaks on it and season them lightly with black pepper. Cook under a moderately hot grill for 3-5 minutes each side, depending on thickness, until the flesh flakes easily and is opaque at the centre. Meanwhile, heat the pepper sauce gently in a small pan.

5 Lift the halibut onto individual warmed serving plates and spread a spoonful of the sauce alongside each steak; garnish with the sprigs of parsley.

Grilled steaks of this meaty, close-textured flatfish are low in calories but substantial. Here, a lively, easily made red-pepper sauce spiced with vinegar enhances the mild flavour of the halibut and moistens its firm flesh.

Baked monkfish

ONE SERVING

CALORIES 235

TOTAL FAT 5g

SATURATED FAT 1g

CARBOHYDRATES 20g

ADDED-SUGAR 0

FIBRE 2g

SODIUM 270mg

SERVES 4
PREPARATION TIME: 15 minutes
COOKING TIME: 40 minutes
OVEN: Preheat to 220°C (425°F, gas mark 7)

½ level teaspoon black peppercorns
1½ lb (680g) monkfish tail, skinned
1lb (450g) potatoes, peeled and thinly sliced
1 large red onion, peeled and finely chopped
1 level teaspoon crumbled dried fennel

1 tablespoon olive oil
Juice of ½ lemon
1 bay leaf

1 Crush the peppercorns roughly in a mortar, or fold them in greaseproof paper and crush them with a rolling pin. Sprinkle the pepper over the monkfish and press it into the flesh.

2 Line an ovenproof dish with a large piece of nonstick baking paper. Arrange a thin layer of potato slices on it, cover them with half the onion, then sprinkle with half the fennel. Lay the monkfish on the vegetables, brush it with the oil and sprinkle on the lemon juice. Cover with the rest of the vegetables and fennel, and add the bay leaf. Fold the paper over closely and tuck under the ends to make a parcel.

3 Cook in the heated oven for 30 minutes, then open the parcel and cook for 5-10 minutes more, until lightly browned. Take out the bay leaf and lift the fish and vegetables onto a warmed serving plate.

A dish of hot ratatouille or a green salad contrasts with the firm fish. You can cook steaks of cod and haddock in the same way.

A favourite fish of Mediterranean Europe, monkfish has just a hint of sweetness, which is lightly echoed in this dish by the fennel.

Fish pie

ONE SERVING

CALORIES 260

TOTAL FAT 5g

SATURATED FAT 2g

CARBOHYDRATES 29g

ADDED SUGAR 0

FIBRE 4g

SODIUM 210mg

SERVES 4
PREPARATION TIME: 50 minutes
COOKING TIME: 30 minutes
OVEN: Preheat to 200°C (400°F, gas mark 6)

1lb (450g) potatoes, peeled and thickly sliced
8oz (225g) carrots, peeled and thickly sliced
Large pinch saffron threads
¾ pint (425ml) water
Freshly ground black pepper
2 level tablespoons low-fat natural yoghurt
2 level tablespoons chopped fresh parsley

For the filling:
24 fresh mussels, scrubbed and scraped
½ oz (15g) slightly salted butter
1 large leek, sliced thinly and washed
4 tablespoons water
1 level tablespoon cornflour mixed to a thin paste with 2 teaspoons water
12oz (340g) coley fillet, skinned and cubed
2 tomatoes, skinned, de-seeded and chopped

1 Put the potatoes and carrots in a large saucepan, with the saffron, and pour in the water. Bring to the boil then reduce the heat, cover and simmer for about 20 minutes, until tender. Drain and keep the cooking liquid.

2   Return the pan of vegetables to a gentle heat and stir constantly for 1-2 minutes until quite dry. Mash thoroughly, then beat in a little pepper and the yoghurt and parsley. Set aside.

3   Pour the reserved vegetable liquid into a saucepan with the mussels. Cover and cook over a high heat, shaking the pan frequently, for 3-4 minutes. Remove the mussels from their shells. Discard any that do not open. Strain the cooking liquid through a sieve lined with kitchen paper into a measuring jug and make it up to ½ pint (285ml) with water if necessary.

4   Melt the butter in a saucepan, toss the leek in it until coated, then add the tablespoons of water and cook, covered, over a gentle heat for 5 minutes until tender. Pour in the reserved cooking liquid and bring to simmering point. Mix in the cornflour paste and cook, stirring, for 2-3 minutes, until the sauce thickens, then take off the heat.

5   Stir the mussels, coley and tomatoes into the sauce and pour into a deep ovenproof dish. Spread the potato mixture evenly on top and crisscross with a fork. Bake the pie in the heated oven for 30 minutes, until golden brown.

Serve in shell dishes. Steamed curly kale or spinach goes well with the pie.

> **TIP**
> *After scrubbing and scraping the mussels, soak them for an hour in cold water sprinkled with a little flour; this helps to clear them of grit.*

Smooth potato, tinged golden with carrot and saffron, covers a blend of succulent white fish and mussels to make a crisply topped pie.

Stuffed plaice with nutmeg sauce

SERVES 4
PREPARATION TIME: 20 minutes
COOKING TIME: 25 minutes
OVEN: Preheat to 180°C (350°F, gas mark 4)

1 tablespoon olive oil
1 large spring onion, trimmed and chopped
1 small carrot, peeled and grated
3oz (85g) cooked brown rice
½ level teaspoon finely grated lemon rind
1 teaspoon lemon juice
¼ level teaspoon freshly grated nutmeg
Freshly ground black pepper
4 plaice double fillets, each about 6oz
(175g), skinned
Wooden cocktail sticks to secure
Fine strips of lemon rind to garnish
8 cooked new carrots to garnish
4 spring onion curls

ONE SERVING

CALORIES 270

TOTAL FAT 10g

SATURATED FAT 1g

CARBOHYDRATES 14g

ADDED SUGAR 0

FIBRE 0

SODIUM 220mg

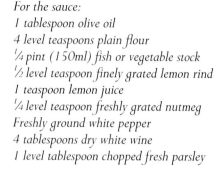

For the sauce:
1 tablespoon olive oil
4 level teaspoons plain flour
¼ pint (150ml) fish or vegetable stock
½ level teaspoon finely grated lemon rind
1 teaspoon lemon juice
¼ level teaspoon freshly grated nutmeg
Freshly ground white pepper
4 tablespoons dry white wine
1 level tablespoon chopped fresh parsley

1 Heat the oil in a saucepan and cook the onion and carrot in it gently for 3-5 minutes, until just tender. Remove from the heat and stir in the rice, lemon rind and juice, and nutmeg. Season with pepper.

2 Lay the fish fillets skinned side up in a lightly oiled, lidded ovenproof dish and season with pepper. Press a quarter of the rice mixture onto the centre of the head end of each fillet, fold the tail end over the filling and secure with cocktail sticks.

3 Cover and cook the fish in the heated oven for 25 minutes, or until the flesh is opaque.

4 Meanwhile, prepare the sauce. Heat the oil in a saucepan over a moderate heat, stir in the flour and cook for 1-2 minutes, stirring continuously. Gradually blend in the stock, then add the grated lemon rind, lemon juice and nutmeg, and season with white pepper. Bring to the boil, stirring continuously, then simmer for 5 minutes before mixing in the wine and the parsley.

5 Lift the fish carefully onto a heated serving dish, remove the cocktail sticks and garnish with the strips of lemon rind, carrots and spring onion curls. Stir the juices from the fish into the sauce and reheat to serve.

Serve the plaice with fine green beans and steamed potatoes or hot crusty rolls.

When freshly grated, nutmeg has no trace of bitterness. Here, it lends its distinctive flavour to both filling and sauce, but with a lightness to match that of the plaice.

Plaice and vegetable parcels

ONE SERVING

CALORIES 195

TOTAL FAT 9g

SATURATED FAT 2g

CARBOHYDRATES 2g

ADDED SUGAR 0

FIBRE 1g

SODIUM 230mg

SERVES 4
PREPARATION TIME: 15 minutes
COOKING TIME: 10 minutes
OVEN: Preheat to 200°C (400°F, gas mark 6)

1 rounded teaspoon finely snipped fresh chives
1 teaspoon lemon juice
½ level teaspoon paprika
1oz (30g) polyunsaturated margarine

1 small red pepper, de-seeded and thinly sliced
2 large spring onions, trimmed and sliced diagonally
4oz (115g) thin asparagus, trimmed and sliced diagonally
1 small courgette, trimmed and thinly sliced diagonally
4 plaice double fillets, each about 5oz (150g), skinned
4 thin slices lemon

Tender white plaice and crisp, colourful vegetables mingle their juices while cooking and release strong, fresh aromas as the steaming parcels are unwrapped.

1 Work the chives, lemon juice and paprika into the margarine with a knife and set aside.

2 Boil the vegetables for 1 minute in just enough water to cover. Drain and set aside.

3 Cut 4 pieces of nonstick baking paper, each large enough to enclose one plaice fillet. Lay a fillet on each sheet, skinned side down. Spoon a quarter of the vegetables onto each fillet and top the vegetables with a quarter of the chive mixture and a slice of lemon. Fold the edges of the baking paper together over the fish and fold the ends over before tucking them beneath the fish to make secure parcels.

4 Lift the parcels carefully into a baking dish and cook in the heated oven for 10 minutes.

Serve the parcels for the diners to open. Crusty bread and a leafy salad go well with the plaice in summer, while baked garlic potatoes make a satisfying winter accompaniment. You can use sole or flounder instead of plaice.

Skate vinaigrette

Tenderised by the vinegar in the poaching liquid, but holding its firm shape, skate is ideal for salads. The capers and dressing give an extra piquancy in this dish.

SERVES 4
PREPARATION TIME: 25 minutes
COOKING TIME: 25 minutes

1¾ lb (800g) skate wings, rinsed and sticky film removed
8fl oz (225ml) vinegar
7oz (200g) onions, peeled and sliced
5 sprigs parsley
1 sprig thyme
1 bay leaf
8oz (225g) lamb's lettuce, washed and drained
1 level tablespoon chopped fresh parsley
1 level tablespoon chopped fresh chervil
2 shallots, peeled and chopped, or 2 spring onions, trimmed and chopped
1 level tablespoon capers, drained
1 tomato, skinned, de-seeded and diced
12 leaves flat-leaf parsley
4 tablespoons vinaigrette dressing

1 Place the skate wings, cut if necessary, in a large saucepan. Pour on 1¾ pints (1 litre) of water and the vinegar. Add the onions, sprigs of parsley and thyme, and the bay leaf. Bring to the boil, then reduce to a simmer and poach very gently, uncovered, for about 25 minutes or until the fish is tender.

2 Meanwhile, spread the lamb's lettuce on a serving dish and sprinkle with the chopped parsley, chervil and shallots or spring onions.

3 Drain the skate and remove the skin. Lift the flesh from the bones and arrange it on the salad. Scatter the capers, tomato and parsley leaves over the fish. Sprinkle on the vinaigrette dressing and serve immediately.

> **TIP**
> **To remove the sticky film from the skate wings, brush them gently with a clean, soft-bristled brush, rinsing frequently under cold running water.**

Lemon sole with sesame seeds

SERVES 4
PREPARATION TIME: 15 minutes,
plus 30 minutes to set
COOKING TIME: 4 minutes

3 level tablespoons plain flour
6 level tablespoons sesame seeds

2 level teaspoons Dijon mustard
2 level teaspoons tomato purée
½ level teaspoon dried tarragon
2fl oz (60ml) semi-skimmed milk
4 lemon sole fillets, each about 5oz (150g), skinned
1 tablespoon olive oil
Lemon slices to garnish

Feather-light fillets of grilled sole are given more substance in this dish by their savoury, crunchy coating of mustard and sesame seeds. Two colourful vegetables complete a summer treat.

1 Mix the flour and sesame seeds together thoroughly and spread the mixture evenly on a dinner plate.

2 Combine the mustard with the tomato purée on a saucer, crumble on the tarragon and mix into the paste.

3 Pour the milk onto a wide dish or plate. Dip one fillet into the milk then turn it over. Spread half a teaspoon of the mustard mixture over the upper side of the fillet then lay the fillet, spread side down, on the sesame mixture. Spread the other side of the fillet with mustard mixture and turn it over into the sesame mixture. Lift the coated fillet onto a large dish.

4 Prepare the other fillets in the same way, then cover the dish and put in the refrigerator for 30 minutes for the coating to set.

5 Line the grill pan with foil and brush the rack with olive oil. Arrange the fillets on the rack, brush lightly with oil and cook under a hot grill for 2 minutes. Turn the fillets over carefully, brush lightly with oil and grill for a further 2 minutes. Lower the heat if the sesame seeds brown too quickly. Lift the fish carefully onto a heated serving dish and garnish with the lemon slices.

Serve the sole with tomatoes and mangetout for sweet and colourful accompaniments.

Stuffed whiting

TIP

To scale a fish, put it inside a large polythene bag and hold it firmly by the tail. Scrape the back of a small knife from the tail down to the head until all the scales are off.

SERVES 4
PREPARATION TIME: 15 minutes
COOKING TIME: 30 minutes
OVEN: Preheat to 200°C (400°F, gas mark 6)

1 tablespoon olive oil
2 medium onions, peeled and finely chopped
1 clove garlic, peeled and finely chopped
1½ oz (45g) fresh white breadcrumbs
2 level tablespoons chopped fresh parsley
Finely grated rind of 1 lemon
Freshly ground black pepper
4 whole whiting, each about 8oz (225g), scaled and cleaned
Wooden cocktail sticks to secure
5 tablespoons dry white wine
Sprigs of flat-leaf parsley to garnish

1 Heat the oil in a frying pan and cook half the onion in it over a moderate heat for about 5 minutes, until soft. Remove from the heat, mix in the garlic, breadcrumbs, parsley and lemon rind and season with pepper.

2 Stuff each whiting with a quarter of the mixture and seal in the stuffing by threading wooden cocktail sticks through the belly flaps.

3 Scatter half the remaining onion in a large ovenproof dish. Arrange the fish in one layer on top and scatter on the rest of the onion. Pour in the wine, then cover the dish with a lid or foil. Cook in the heated oven for 30 minutes or until the fish flakes easily when tested with a fork. Remove the cocktail sticks and garnish with the sprigs of parsley.

Mashed potatoes, browned in the oven while the fish is cooking, and runner beans go well with the whiting. If you cannot buy whole fish, use fillets and secure them round the stuffing with cocktail sticks.

The delicate, small-flaked whiting flesh, so easy to digest, gives its juices to the filling and stays moist in the white wine that lends the dish a sharp edge.

Oatmeal herrings

SERVES 4
PREPARATION TIME: 15 minutes
COOKING TIME: 15 minutes
OVEN: Preheat to 180°C (350°F, gas mark 4)

2oz (60g) cooked brown rice
2oz (60g) medium oatmeal
1oz (30g) finely grated Cheddar cheese
2 level teaspoons chopped or snipped fresh chives
1 small tomato, finely chopped
2 level teaspoons whole-grain mustard
2 level teaspoons quark or low-fat natural yoghurt
Freshly ground black pepper
4 herrings, each about 8oz (225g), gutted and
cleaned, heads and bones removed
Wooden cocktail sticks for securing
Sprigs of flat-leaf parsley to garnish

1 Mix the rice with half the oatmeal, the
Cheddar, chives, tomato, mustard and quark
or yoghurt to make a well-blended stuffing.
Season with pepper.

2 Wash the herrings and pat dry with kitchen
paper. Fill each with a quarter of the stuffing
and pin the edges together securely with
cocktail sticks threaded along the belly flaps.

3 Sprinkle half the remaining oatmeal into a
shallow ovenproof dish and lay the herrings on
top in a single layer. Sprinkle with the rest of
the oatmeal.

4 Cook, uncovered, in the heated oven for
about 15 minutes, until the flesh flakes easily
when tested with a fork. Lift the herrings
carefully onto warmed dinner plates, remove
the cocktail sticks and garnish with the parsley.

*In the days when the fishing fleets of Scotland and
northern England spilled out copious catches of
silvery herring, the fish were everyday fare. Now
they are less common and paradoxically more
appreciated for their succulent flesh, which is kept
moist during cooking by its own oil.*

Swede, carrot and potato purée
makes a traditional north-country winter
accompaniment to the herrings, and a
watercress salad adds its own peppery quality to
the robust flavours of the dish.

ONE SERVING	
CALORIES	400
TOTAL FAT	27g
SATURATED FAT	8g
CARBOHYDRATES	16g
ADDED SUGAR	0
FIBRE	2g
SODIUM	195mg

Soused herrings

ONE SERVING

CALORIES 340

TOTAL FAT 25g

    SATURATED FAT 7g

CARBOHYDRATES 4g

    ADDED SUGAR 0

FIBRE 1g

SODIUM 320mg

SERVES 4

PREPARATION TIME: 20 minutes, plus 1-2 days to marinate

COOKING TIME: 15 minutes

OVEN: Preheat to 180°C (350°F, gas mark 4)

½ pint (285ml) cider vinegar
½ pint (285ml) water
3 juniper berries
6 cloves
¼ level teaspoon ground allspice

6 black peppercorns, lightly crushed
1 bay leaf
4 herrings, each about 8oz (225g), scaled, heads removed, gutted and boned
4 level teaspoons English mustard powder
2 teaspoons water
2 small red onions, peeled, thinly sliced and separated into rings
1 level tablespoon pickled capers, drained
2 small dill-pickled cucumbers, halved lengthways
Wooden cocktail sticks

Richly spiced and sharpened by the mustard and capers, these plump, home-pickled herrings re-create a traditional Scandinavian delicacy.

1 Bring the vinegar, water, juniper berries, cloves, allspice, peppercorns and bay leaf to the boil in a stainless steel or enamel pan, then simmer, uncovered, for 10 minutes. Set aside.

2 Rinse the herrings, pat them dry with kitchen paper and lay them, skin side down, on a board covered with greaseproof paper. Mix the mustard with the water, spread a quarter of the mixture on each fish and arrange a few onion rings and capers on top. Lay a piece of pickled cucumber across the head end of each fillet, and roll up from head to tail. Secure each roll with a cocktail stick.

3 Pack the herrings snugly into an ovenproof glass or china dish and scatter the remaining onion rings on top. Pour the spiced vinegar over the fish. Cover the dish and bake in the heated oven for about 15 minutes, or until the flesh just begins to flake when tested with the tip of a knife. Leave to cool.

4 Remove the cocktail sticks and put the covered dish of herrings in the refrigerator for 1-2 days to 'souse'.

Potato salad, crisp lamb's lettuce and tomatoes are foils for the sharp taste of the herrings.

Fisherman's mackerel

SERVES 4
PREPARATION TIME: 5 minutes
COOKING TIME: 15 minutes

8 mackerel fillets, each about 4oz (115g)
Freshly ground black pepper
2 tablespoons lemon juice
Sprigs of fresh dill and lemon wedges to garnish

1 Rinse the mackerel and pat dry with kitchen paper. Season on both sides with pepper.

2 Line the grill pan with foil. Arrange the opened mackerel skin side down on the grill rack. Grill under a moderate heat without turning for 10-15 minutes, according to their thickness. The flesh should flake easily and be very slightly browned; do not overcook or the fish will be dry.

3 Turn the mackerel over one by one onto a warmed plate, peel off the skins, then arrange them, grilled side up, on a warmed serving dish and sprinkle with the lemon juice. Garnish with the sprigs of dill and lemon wedges.

ONE SERVING	
CALORIES	335
TOTAL FAT	27g
SATURATED FAT	5g
CARBOHYDRATES	0
ADDED SUGAR	0
FIBRE	0
SODIUM	215mg

Fresh mackerel fillets are often overlooked in favour of smoked – a pity, since they are quick to cook and satisfyingly rich to eat because of the oils they contain.

Mackerel with hot sour sauce

SERVES 4
PREPARATION TIME: 20 minutes
COOKING TIME: 15 minutes

1½ tablespoons olive oil
2 level teaspoons peeled and grated root ginger
1 clove garlic, peeled and crushed
1 shallot, peeled and finely chopped
1 medium carrot, peeled and cut into strips
4 miniature sweetcorn cobs, trimmed and sliced
1oz (30g) mangetout, trimmed and
sliced diagonally
3 level tablespoons cornflour
7fl oz (200ml) red wine vinegar
2 tablespoons clear honey

1 tablespoon soy sauce
4 mackerel, each about 7oz (200g), gutted,
cleaned and heads removed
Fresh dill fronds to garnish

1 Heat 1 tablespoon of the oil in a saucepan and cook the ginger, garlic and shallot in it gently for 1 minute, stirring occasionally. Mix in the carrot, sweetcorn and mangetout and cook for 2 minutes, then set aside.

2 Blend 1 tablespoon of the cornflour with the vinegar, then stir in the honey and soy sauce.

3 Wash and dry the mackerel. Brush them with the rest of the oil and dust with the remaining cornflour. Slash them in three or four places on both sides.

4 Line the grill pan with foil and place the mackerel on the rack. Cook for 5-6 minutes on each side under a hot grill, until the skin is crisp and brown and the flesh just firm. If the skin browns too quickly, lower the heat.

5 Meanwhile, stir the vinegar mixture into the vegetables in the saucepan and bring to the boil, stirring continuously. Reduce the heat and cook for 1 minute. Lift the mackerel onto heated individual serving plates, spoon the sauce round and garnish with dill. Leave the diners to remove the skin for themselves.

The sauce gives the mackerel the taste of the East, and Chinese noodles sprinkled with spring onion make an authentic accompaniment.

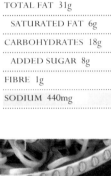

ONE SERVING	
CALORIES	455
TOTAL FAT	31g
SATURATED FAT	6g
CARBOHYDRATES	18g
ADDED SUGAR	8g
FIBRE	1g
SODIUM	440mg

Red mullet with leeks and tomatoes

ONE SERVING	
CALORIES	205
TOTAL FAT	6g
SATURATED FAT	1g
CARBOHYDRATES	3g
ADDED SUGAR	0
FIBRE	2g
SODIUM	220mg

SERVES 6
PREPARATION TIME: 25 minutes,
plus 30 minutes to marinate
COOKING TIME: 15 minutes

2 tablespoons olive oil
1 level tablespoon finely chopped fresh rosemary

Freshly ground black pepper
6 large whole fresh red mullet (or frozen mullet, thawed), each about 10oz (275g), scaled and gutted
3 small leeks, trimmed, thinly sliced and washed
3 large tomatoes, skinned, de-seeded and chopped
Lemon wedges and fresh rosemary sprigs to garnish

1 Smear a large dish with 1 tablespoon of the oil, sprinkle in the chopped rosemary and season with pepper. Rinse the mullet, pat dry with kitchen paper and arrange them in the dish in one layer. Turn them until evenly coated with rosemary. Cover and leave to marinate at room temperature for 30 minutes.

2 Meanwhile, heat the remaining olive oil in a frying pan, and cook the leeks over a moderate heat for 6-8 minutes, stirring frequently, until softened. Stir in the tomatoes and bring to the boil. Boil rapidly for 2-3 minutes to evaporate the excess liquid. Leave to cool.

3 Spoon the leek and tomato mixture inside the mullet but do not overfill them. Oil the grill rack, lay the fish on it and cook under a moderate heat for 8-9 minutes. Turn them over carefully and cook for a further 5-6 minutes.

4 Lift the fish onto warmed plates and garnish with the lemon wedges and rosemary sprigs.

Warm french bread and lightly steamed mangetout go well with the fish. When the mullet are small, as they often are, allow two fish for each person.

Simply cooked with herbs and a moist filling, red mullet is a gourmet's delight. Beneath the vivid skin, the flesh is white and delicate in texture, but the flavour is surprisingly full. Choose large fish when you can, to get correspondingly bigger pieces of flesh among the plentiful bones.

Salmon with cucumber and dill sauce

ONE SERVING	
CALORIES	245
TOTAL FAT	15g
SATURATED FAT	3g
CARBOHYDRATES	3g
ADDED SUGAR	0
FIBRE	0
SODIUM	165mg

SERVES 6
PREPARATION TIME: 10 minutes
COOKING TIME: 25 minutes
OVEN: Preheat to 180°C (350°F, gas mark 4)

2lb (900g) middle-cut or tail-end salmon
in one piece
1 small cucumber, peeled, de-seeded and diced
4oz (115g) low-fat natural yoghurt

2 level teaspoons coarsely chopped fresh
dill, or ½ teaspoon dill seeds
1 teaspoon skimmed milk or water
½ level teaspoon made English mustard
Freshly ground white or black pepper
Thinly sliced cucumber and chopped fresh dill
to garnish

1 Lay the salmon in a baking dish lined with
a large piece of foil. Pour in cold water to a
depth of about ½ in (13mm), then bring all the
sides of the foil together to enclose the salmon
and water. Cook in the heated oven for about
25 minutes, or until the salmon is opaque
and flakes easily.

2 Meanwhile, combine the diced cucumber,
yoghurt, chopped dill or dill seeds, milk or
water and mustard, and season with pepper.
Cover the sauce and put in the refrigerator.

3 Unwrap the salmon, lift it carefully onto a
serving plate and remove the skin. Cut into the
fish horizontally along the sides as far as the
spine, and lift off the upper part of the flesh.
Remove the bones and replace the flesh.

Garnish the salmon with cucumber slices and
dill, and serve it warm or cold with the sauce.
New potatoes or wholemeal bread, and a leafy
salad are simple foils for this summer treat.

*Dill gives the sauce a warm, sweet taste similar to
caraway. Combined with the freshness of cucumber, it
makes a perfect complement to the rich salmon.*

Salmon fish cakes

ONE SERVING	
CALORIES	360
TOTAL FAT	17g
SATURATED FAT	3g
CARBOHYDRATES	29g
ADDED SUGAR	0
FIBRE	3g
SODIUM	240mg

SERVES 4
PREPARATION TIME: 30 minutes
COOKING TIME: 10 minutes

11oz (300g) potatoes, peeled
12oz (340g) salmon steaks
2 level tablespoons low-fat natural yoghurt
1 beaten egg, size 2
1 medium carrot, peeled and finely grated

1 large onion, peeled and finely chopped
½ level teaspoon paprika
1 teaspoon lemon juice
2oz (60g) fine wholemeal breadcrumbs
1½ tablespoons corn oil
Lemon wedges and chervil sprigs to garnish

1 Put the potatoes in boiling water and cook
for 8-10 minutes, until tender.

2 Meanwhile, line the grill pan with foil, lay the salmon steaks on the rack and grill for 2-3 minutes on each side, until opaque all through. Skin and bone the steaks and flake the flesh.

3 Mash the potatoes without milk or fat. Turn them into a bowl and mix in the salmon, yoghurt, egg, carrot, onion, paprika and lemon juice. Divide the mixture into eight and shape each piece into a flat cake.

4 Spread the crumbs on a plate and lay two or three cakes at a time on it. Use a spoon and palette knife to press crumbs gently onto the top and sides of the cakes.

5 Heat the oil in a large nonstick frying pan and fry the fish cakes in it over a moderate heat for 3 minutes on each side, until golden brown.

Serve the salmon fish cakes garnished with the lemon wedges and chervil. A mixed leafy salad makes a fittingly crisp accompaniment. Instead of making the cakes with salmon, you can use 7oz (200g) of tinned tuna, drained of oil.

Soft pink salmon inside a crust of crisp golden crumbs makes fish cakes that are the focus of a filling meal. Although substantial, the cakes are surprisingly light and go well with salads.

Grating horseradish for the sauce may bring tears to your eyes, but it gives an unmistakable piquancy to this simple dish of grilled salmon.

Grilled salmon with horseradish sauce

ONE SERVING	
CALORIES	270
TOTAL FAT	18g
SATURATED FAT	4g
CARBOHYDRATES	4g
ADDED SUGAR	0
FIBRE	0
SODIUM	160mg

SERVES 4
PREPARATION TIME: 5 minutes
COOKING TIME: 5 minutes

5oz (150g) Greek yoghurt
5oz (150g) low-fat natural yoghurt
3 spring onions, trimmed and chopped
10 radishes, washed and chopped
3 level tablespoons freshly grated horseradish
½ level teaspoon ground cumin
Freshly ground black pepper
1 tablespoon olive oil
4 salmon steaks, each about 4oz (115g)
1 tablespoon lemon juice

1 To make the sauce, mix the yoghurts, onions, radishes, horseradish, cumin and pepper in a bowl. Cover and refrigerate.

2 Line the grill pan with foil, oil the rack and heat the grill. Rinse and dry the salmon and lay on the rack. Mix the remaining oil with the lemon juice, season with pepper and trickle half the mixture over the steaks. Cook under a medium grill for 2-3 minutes, until lightly browned. Turn the steaks over, trickle the remaining oil mixture over them and grill for a further 2-3 minutes, or until the steaks are opaque right through the centre.

Serve the salmon on warmed plates with a spoonful of the chilled sauce beside each steak. Saffron-tinted rice and steamed courgettes are perfect foils for the rich salmon. If you cannot find fresh horseradish, use 1 level tablespoon of Dijon mustard in the sauce instead, but it will have less character.

Lemon-marinated sardines

SERVES 4
PREPARATION TIME: 20 minutes,
plus 30 minutes to marinate
COOKING TIME: 8 minutes

1 tablespoon olive oil
Juice of 1 lemon
1 clove garlic, peeled and crushed
2 level tablespoons chopped fresh parsley
Freshly ground black pepper
2lb (900g) fresh sardines, scaled and gutted,
washed and dried with kitchen paper
Lemon wedges and parsley sprigs to garnish

1 Mix the oil, lemon juice, garlic and chopped parsley in a wide dish and season with pepper. Turn the fish in the mixture until coated, then cover and leave to marinate for 30 minutes.

2 Line the grill pan with foil and lay the fish on the rack. Cook under a hot grill for about 8 minutes, turning once. Baste frequently with the marinade. Lift the fish carefully onto a warmed serving dish, pour on the juices and garnish with lemon wedges and parsley sprigs.

ONE SERVING	
CALORIES	220
TOTAL FAT	12g
SATURATED FAT	2g
CARBOHYDRATES	0
ADDED SUGAR	0
FIBRE	0
SODIUM	135mg

Fresh sardines are popular in many southern European countries, where they are usually grilled or barbecued. In this recipe, a marinade containing plenty of lemon juice balances the richness of the fish.

Gingered swordfish steaks

SERVES 4
PREPARATION TIME: 10 minutes, plus 2 hours
to marinate
COOKING TIME: 6 minutes

2½ tablespoons olive oil
1 level teaspoon grated lemon rind
2 tablespoons lemon juice
1 tablespoon dry sherry or water
2 teaspoons light soy sauce
2 cloves garlic, peeled and crushed
2 level teaspoons peeled and grated root ginger,
or ¼ level teaspoon ground ginger
Freshly ground black pepper
4 swordfish steaks, about 4oz (115g) each

1 Make the marinade by mixing 2 tablespoons
of the oil, the lemon rind and juice, sherry
or water, soy sauce, garlic and ginger in a bowl.
Season with pepper.

2 Lay the swordfish steaks in a dish in a single
layer. Pour the marinade over the steaks
and turn them to coat well. Cover and put in
the refrigerator for 2 hours to marinate.

3 Heat the remaining oil in a frying pan. Lift
the swordfish steaks out of the marinade and
fry them over a moderate heat for 3 minutes on
each side. Put the fish on a heated serving dish
and pour on the cooking juices.

A salad of apple and lettuce balances the fish's
fieriness, and warm rolls mop up the juices.
You can cook tuna steaks in the same way.

*The marinade tenderises the close-textured
swordfish and gives its strong flavour a sharp, hot
edge. Since the flesh is so firm, the marinated steaks
are suitable for cooking on a barbecue.*

> **TIP**
> **Swordfish is a very
> firm, meaty fish
> that does not flake
> easily. It is cooked
> sufficiently when
> the flesh feels
> springy to the
> touch.**

Trout in herb and wine jelly

SERVES 4
PREPARATION TIME: 45 minutes, plus
at least 4 hours to set and chill
COOKING TIME: 10 minutes

1 pint (570ml) fish stock
4fl oz (115ml) dry white wine
3 tablespoons white wine vinegar
1 large shallot, peeled and finely chopped
½ level teaspoon coarsely ground pink peppercorns
3 tablespoons cold water
1 level tablespoon powdered gelatine
2 rainbow trout, each about 8oz (225g), gutted
and cleaned
1 smoked trout, about 9oz (250g), skin and
all bones removed
2 level tablespoons each chopped fresh parsley,
tarragon and chervil
Flat-leaf parsley sprigs to garnish

1 Pour the stock, wine and vinegar into a large
stainless steel or enamel saucepan with the
shallot and peppercorns, and bring to the boil.
Boil rapidly for 10-15 minutes until the liquid
is reduced to 8fl oz (225ml). Take off the heat.

2 Pour the water into a small saucepan and
sprinkle on the gelatine. Leave for 5 minutes
to swell, then heat very gently to dissolve. Pour
a little of the fish-stock mixture onto the
gelatine and mix well, then stir this liquid
into the bulk of the stock. Leave to cool.

3 Line the grill pan with foil, lay the fresh
trout on the rack and cook them under a high
heat for about 4 minutes on each side, until the
flesh turns opaque and flakes easily when tested
with a fork. Leave to cool, then remove the skin
and all bones.

4 Flake the fresh trout and the smoked trout
into a bowl and gently fold in the parsley,
tarragon and chervil. Stir in the cooled stock
and pour the mixture into a nonstick loaf tin
7½ × 3½ in (19×9cm). Cover and chill for
at least 4 hours until well set.

5 Dip the loaf tin into hot water for
10 seconds, or wrap it in a hot cloth, to loosen
the jellied trout from the sides. Turn it out
onto a serving dish, cut it into eight slices and
garnish it with the parsley sprigs.

ONE SERVING	
CALORIES 180	
TOTAL FAT 5g	
SATURATED FAT 1g	
CARBOHYDRATES 1g	
ADDED SUGAR 0	
FIBRE 0	
SODIUM 140mg	

*A combination of wine and herbs complements
the subtle flavour of the trout to create an elegantly
marbled summer dish. Pink peppercorns and
smoked trout give it extra colour and zest.*

Trout with orange and mint stuffing

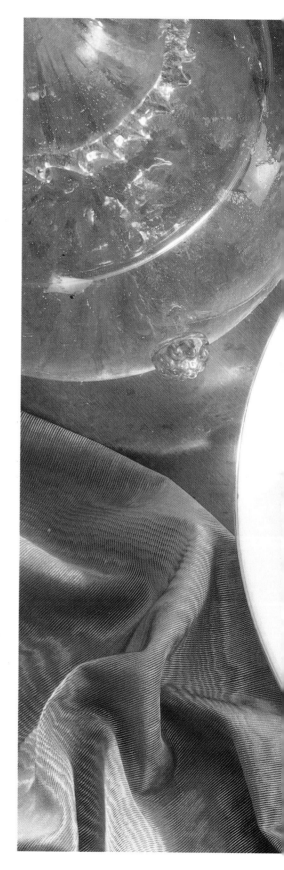

SERVES 4
PREPARATION TIME: 20 minutes
COOKING TIME: 30 minutes
OVEN: Preheat to 180°C (350°F, gas mark 4)

....
ONE SERVING
CALORIES 240
TOTAL FAT 6g
SATURATED FAT 1g
CARBOHYDRATES 17g
ADDED SUGAR 0
FIBRE 2g
SODIUM 230mg
....

2oz (60g) wholemeal breadcrumbs
Finely grated rind of ½ orange
1 small stick celery, trimmed and finely chopped
½ small dessert apple, peeled, cored and diced
3 level teaspoons chopped fresh mint
About 1 tablespoon fromage frais
Freshly ground black pepper
4 rainbow trout, each about 8oz (225g), gutted, cleaned, heads removed, washed and dried
Wooden cocktail sticks to secure
Juice of 1 lemon
Juice of 1 large orange
About ¼ pint (150ml) dry vermouth
1 clove garlic, peeled and crushed
1 shallot, peeled and finely chopped
1 tablespoon chopped fresh parsley
Orange slices and sprigs of fresh mint to garnish

1 Mix the breadcrumbs, orange rind, celery, apple and 1 teaspoon of the mint in a bowl. Stir in enough fromage frais to make a moist, crumbly stuffing. Season with pepper.

2 Fill the cavity in each trout with stuffing and secure with cocktail sticks. Lay the trout in a shallow ovenproof dish.

3 Strain the lemon and orange juice into a measuring jug and make up to ½ pint (285ml) with the vermouth. Stir in the garlic, shallot, chopped parsley and remaining mint.

4 Pour the mixture over the trout. Cover and cook in the heated oven for about 30 minutes, or until the flesh is opaque and flakes easily when tested with a fork.

5 Lift the fish onto a warm serving dish and remove the cocktail sticks. Pour the cooking liquid into a small pan and boil rapidly until reduced to a cupful. Pour it round the trout and garnish with orange slices and mint sprigs.

Serve new potatoes and a watercress salad with the fish. Leave the diners to remove the trout skin for themselves.

TIP
To remove the skin from cooked trout, make a cut right along the back of the fish, lift a corner of the skin at the head end and peel the skin back to the tail.

The tangy, crunchy stuffing and lively vermouth sauce make this colourful fish dish particularly suitable for serving at any special occasion.

Exploit the versatility of tinned tuna by combining it with Indian spices and a mixture of juicy fruits to create this refreshing summer dish.

Curried tuna and fruit

SERVES 4
PREPARATION TIME: 20 minutes, plus 1 hour to chill

4oz (115g) low-fat natural yoghurt
1 level tablespoon mild curry powder
¼ level teaspoon each ground cumin, ground
cardamom and coriander
14oz (400g) tinned tuna, drained of oil, flaked
1 large orange, peel and pith pared off, segments
cut free of membranes and each divided into three
5oz (150g) fresh pineapple, cut into chunks
3oz (85g) each red and green seedless grapes, halved
4oz (115g) water chestnuts, sliced
12 cos lettuce leaves, washed and dried

1 Mix the yoghurt, curry powder, cumin, cardamom and coriander in a large bowl.

2 Gently mix in the tuna, orange, pineapple, grapes and water chestnuts until coated with dressing. Chill in the refrigerator for 1 hour.

3 Arrange the lettuce leaves on individual plates and spoon the tuna and fruit on top.

Serve with crusty rolls or brown rice dressed with lemon juice. You may prefer to peel the grapes and use well-drained unsweetened tinned pineapple in place of fresh.

ONE SERVING	
CALORIES	290
TOTAL FAT	10g
SATURATED FAT	2g
CARBOHYDRATES	22g
ADDED SUGAR	0
FIBRE	3g
SODIUM	340mg

Devilled crab

SERVES 4
PREPARATION TIME: 30 minutes
COOKING TIME: 15 minutes

1oz (30g) polyunsaturated margarine
3 medium spring onions, trimmed and
finely chopped
1 medium stick celery, trimmed and finely chopped
1 level tablespoon plain flour
¼ pint (150ml) skimmed milk
1 level teaspoon Dijon mustard
1 teaspoon lemon juice
¼ level teaspoon cayenne pepper
1lb (450g) cooked fresh crabmeat, white and
brown, roughly chopped
1 level tablespoon chopped fresh parsley
4 level tablespoons dry breadcrumbs

1 Melt half the margarine in a saucepan and
cook the spring onions and celery in it over a
moderate heat for about 5 minutes, until they
are just beginning to soften but not browned.
Blend in the flour and cook for 1 minute.
Gradually stir in the milk and bring to the boil,
stirring continuously, until the sauce is thick
and smooth. Simmer for 2 minutes.

2 Remove the sauce from the heat and
blend in the mustard, lemon juice and cayenne
pepper. Stir in the crabmeat and parsley, and
reheat the sauce to simmering point.

3 Melt the remaining margarine in a small
saucepan without letting it colour, and stir in
the breadcrumbs.

4 Divide the crab mixture between four
scallop shells or individual gratin dishes.
Sprinkle a quarter of the butter and crumb
mixture over the top of each.

5 Cook under a hot grill for 3-4 minutes,
until bubbling hot and golden brown on top,
and serve immediately.

The crunchy vegetables and breadcrumb topping
offer a contrast in texture to the soft crabmeat,
while the parsley and spices add a peppery spark.

A pasta salad or crusty bread and a leafy salad
will go well with this dish. In place of the fresh
crab you can use tinned crab, well drained, or
frozen crabmeat completely thawed.

ONE SERVING	
CALORIES	235
TOTAL FAT	8g
SATURATED FAT	1g
CARBOHYDRATES	10g
ADDED SUGAR	0
FIBRE	0
SODIUM	610mg

Souffléed Brixham crab

SERVES 4
PREPARATION TIME: 15 minutes
COOKING TIME: 20 minutes
OVEN: Preheat to 190°C (375°F, gas mark 5)

1oz (30g) slightly salted butter
4 level tablespoons dried breadcrumbs
1oz (30g) plain flour
¼ pint (150ml) skimmed milk
¼ pint (150ml) fish stock
Juice and finely grated rind of ½ small lemon
¼ teaspoon anchovy essence
1½ level teaspoons paprika
8oz (225g) fresh crabmeat, chopped
4 egg whites, size 2

1 Lightly butter four gratin dishes 6in (15cm) in diameter and sprinkle with the breadcrumbs.

2 Melt the remaining butter in a saucepan, stir in the flour and gradually blend in the milk and stock. Bring to the boil, stirring, then simmer for 2 minutes. Mix in the lemon juice and rind, anchovy essence, paprika and crabmeat.

3 Whisk the egg whites until they hold soft peaks. Using a metal spoon, fold the whites gently into the crab sauce and divide the mixture between the prepared dishes.

4 Bake in the heated oven for 20 minutes, until well risen but still creamy in the centre.

Warm rolls and a mixed bean salad make satisfying accompaniments. You can use frozen and thawed crab in place of fresh, and use one wide, shallow dish if you prefer.

ONE SERVING	
CALORIES	200
TOTAL FAT	7g
SATURATED FAT	4g
CARBOHYDRATES	14g
ADDED SUGAR	0
FIBRE	0
SODIUM	450mg

TIP
When preparing a fresh crab, use a long skewer or a clean knitting needle to get all the meat out of the claws and crevices.

The sea around Devon abounds with crabs, and some of the largest are landed at Brixham. In this dish, crabmeat sits in a buttery crumb coating and is swathed in a fluffy sauce.

Spiced prawns

SERVES 4
PREPARATION TIME: 20 minutes, plus 4 hours
to refrigerate
COOKING TIME: 10 minutes

2 tablespoons olive oil
1½ lb (680g) frozen, uncooked freshwater prawns,
thawed, peeled and de-veined
2 spring onions, trimmed, green part finely sliced,
white part chopped
2 level teaspoons peeled and grated root ginger,
or ¼ level teaspoon ground ginger
¼ pint (150ml) fish stock
2 tablespoons tomato purée
2 tablespoons dry sherry
2 tablespoons cider vinegar
¼ level teaspoon cayenne pepper
8 cos lettuce leaves, washed and patted dry

ONE SERVING

CALORIES 140

TOTAL FAT 8g

SATURATED FAT 1g

CARBOHYDRATES 1g

ADDED SUGAR 0

FIBRE 0

SODIUM 175mg

1 Heat half the oil in a frying pan and stir-fry the prawns in it over a moderate heat for 2 minutes. Spoon into a dish.

2 Heat the remaining oil in the pan, and stir-fry the white onion and ginger for 30 seconds. Stir in the stock, tomato purée, sherry, vinegar and cayenne pepper. Simmer for 3 minutes.

3 Return the prawns to the pan and cook for 3 minutes, stirring. Add half the green onion and pour the prawns and sauce into a bowl. Cool, then cover and refrigerate for 4 hours.

4 Arrange the lettuce on four plates, spoon in the prawns and scatter on the remaining onion.

Serve with brown rice and lamb's lettuce. You can use cooked and peeled North Atlantic prawns but their salt content is much higher.

Crisp lettuce leaves hold cool prawns, but in the sherry sauce there are sparks of fire, given by ginger and cayenne pepper.

Scallops with creamed celeriac

SERVES 4
PREPARATION TIME: 20 minutes
COOKING TIME: 25 minutes

1½ lb (680g) celeriac, peeled and grated
14oz (400g) potatoes, peeled and diced
Freshly ground black pepper
15 bay leaves
1 level tablespoon peeled and grated root ginger
16 fresh scallops, washed and wiped
½ oz (15g) slightly salted butter
1 tablespoon lemon juice
Fresh dill fronds and lemon rind to garnish

1 Cook the celeriac and potatoes in a steamer for about 15 minutes, or until they are tender, then pass them through a vegetable mill or sieve into a heatproof bowl. Thin the mixture with a little of the cooking water if necessary, and beat with a fork to make a fluffy purée.

Season well with pepper. Cover the bowl and stand it over a saucepan of hot water.

2 Line the steamer with the bay leaves, sprinkle on the grated ginger and lay the scallops on top. Cover and steam for 6-7 minutes, until the scallops turn opaque and are tender when pierced with a fork.

3 Melt the butter in a saucepan and stir in the lemon juice. Spoon the potato and celeriac purée neatly onto four warmed plates and arrange the scallops beside it. Pour the lemon butter over the scallops, sprinkle with pepper and garnish with the dill and lemon rind.

Serve immediately with lightly cooked fine green beans or a green salad. You can vary the dish by using large raw prawns or cubes of halibut in place of the scallops.

Lightly steamed scallops have a tender flesh, well matched by a light vegetable purée which is given a mildly peppery flavour here by the celeriac. The orange corals of the scallops add colour to the dish.

Stir-fried squid and vegetables

SERVES 4
PREPARATION TIME: 30 minutes
COOKING TIME: 5 minutes

3 medium squid, each about 6oz (175g), cleaned, tentacle cluster left whole, body cut into thin rings
1 egg white, size 4

2 level teaspoons cornflour
2 tablespoons olive oil
4fl oz (115ml) fish stock or water
6oz (175g) broccoli florets
1 clove garlic, peeled and finely chopped
2 level teaspoons peeled and grated root ginger,
or ¼ teaspoon ground ginger

1 level teaspoon finely chopped clementine or orange rind
2 tablespoons dry sherry
1 level tablespoon black-bean sauce
1 level tablespoon oyster sauce
6oz (175g) mangetout, trimmed and sliced
4oz (115g) peeled prawns

1 Mix the squid with the egg white and half the cornflour.

2 Heat half the oil in a wok until very hot and stir-fry the squid in it for about 1 minute, until opaque. Spoon into a warmed dish.

3 Keep 1 teaspoon of the fish stock or water and bring the rest to the boil in a small saucepan. Cook the broccoli in it for 1 minute. Drain thoroughly, reserving the liquid.

4 Heat the remaining oil in the wok and stir-fry the garlic, ginger and clementine or orange rind for about 30 seconds. Stir in the reserved cooking liquid, the sherry, black-bean sauce and oyster sauce and bring to the boil. Mix the remaining cornflour with the reserved teaspoon of stock or water and blend it into the wok. Cook, stirring, until thickened.

5 Return the squid to the wok and add the broccoli, mangetout and prawns. Cook, stirring, for 1-2 minutes until all the ingredients are hot, and serve at once.

Steamed white rice is the best companion for the dish, and a light side salad of cucumber and tomatoes is refreshing. Instead of cleaning and preparing the squid, you can buy 12oz (340g) of prepared squid rings from a fishmonger.

Oriental-style batter makes the squid crisp but not heavy, and oyster sauce intensifies the seafood's flavour in this colourful dish.

Seafood gumbo

SERVES 6
PREPARATION TIME: 20 minutes
COOKING TIME: 1 hour 15 minutes

ONE SERVING

CALORIES 305

TOTAL FAT 7g

SATURATED FAT 1g

CARBOHYDRATES 35g

ADDED SUGAR 0

FIBRE 3g

SODIUM 490mg

2 tablespoons olive oil
2 medium onions, peeled and chopped
1 clove garlic, peeled and crushed
1 small green pepper, de-seeded and chopped
1 stick celery, trimmed and chopped
2 level tablespoons plain flour
1¼ pints (725ml) fish stock
14oz (400g) tinned chopped tomatoes

3oz (85g) cooked ham, chopped
1 bay leaf
¼ teaspoon Tabasco
8oz (225g) fresh okra, trimmed and sliced
6oz (175g) long-grain rice
8oz (225g) raw freshwater prawns, peeled and de-veined
8oz (225g) fresh white crabmeat, chopped
12 fresh oysters, shelled

1 Heat the oil in a heavy, flameproof casserole and cook the onions in it over a moderate heat for 5 minutes. Mix in the garlic, pepper and celery and cook, stirring often, for 5 minutes.

2 Sprinkle on the flour and cook, stirring, for 1 minute. Stir in the stock, tomatoes, ham, bay leaf and Tabasco. Bring to the boil, partially cover and simmer for 30 minutes. Add the okra and cook, covered, for another 30 minutes.

3 Meanwhile, cook the rice.

4 Stir the prawns and crabmeat into the gumbo and cook for about 2 minutes until the prawns are pink. Add the oysters and cook for 1 minute more. Remove the bay leaf.

Ladle the gumbo into bowls, and give each one a serving of the rice. You can use frozen okra if fresh okra is not available.

Gumbo is another name for okra pods, whose sticky juice thickens this Caribbean fish stew.

Californian seafood stew

SERVES 4
PREPARATION TIME: 15 minutes
COOKING TIME: 55 minutes

ONE SERVING

CALORIES 235

TOTAL FAT 6g

SATURATED FAT 1g

CARBOHYDRATES 8g

ADDED SUGAR 0

FIBRE 2g

SODIUM 320mg

1 tablespoon olive oil
1 large onion, peeled and chopped
3 cloves garlic, peeled and crushed
1 green pepper, de-seeded and cut into strips
¼ pint (150ml) water
14oz (400g) tinned chopped tomatoes
½ pint (285ml) fish or vegetable stock
3½ fl oz (100ml) dry white wine

½ level teaspoon mild chilli powder
½ level teaspoon each dried oregano, thyme and marjoram
1 bay leaf
16 fresh mussels, well scrubbed and scraped clean
8oz (225g) haddock, skinned, boned and cut into cubes
5oz (150g) fresh scallops, cleaned
8oz (225g) raw freshwater prawns, peeled and de-veined
8 large unpeeled cooked prawns to garnish
2 level tablespoons chopped fresh parsley to garnish

1 Heat the oil in a large, heavy-based saucepan. Stir in the onion, garlic, pepper and 2 tablespoons of the water and cook over a moderate heat for about 7 minutes, stirring frequently, until the onion begins to colour.

2 Add the tomatoes, remaining water, stock, wine, chilli powder, dried herbs and bay leaf. Cover and simmer for 45 minutes.

3 Put in the mussels and simmer for 1 minute. Mix in the haddock, scallops and raw prawns.

Cook over a low heat for 3-5 minutes, until the mussels have opened. Discard the bay leaf and garnish the stew with the unpeeled prawns and chopped parsley before taking to the table.

Serve this hearty stew in bowls with plenty of crusty bread to soak up the juices. A cucumber salad afterwards refreshes the palate. You can use cod or halibut in place of the haddock, and frozen rather than fresh peeled prawns; these need only be rinsed, not thawed, before being put in the stew.

TIP
When scrubbing mussels, tap the shells and discard any mussels that do not immediately close. After cooking, discard any that have not opened.

Tomatoes and wine, spiked with chilli powder and herbs, produce a rich broth in which fruits of the sea are poached to make a vivid, savoury stew.

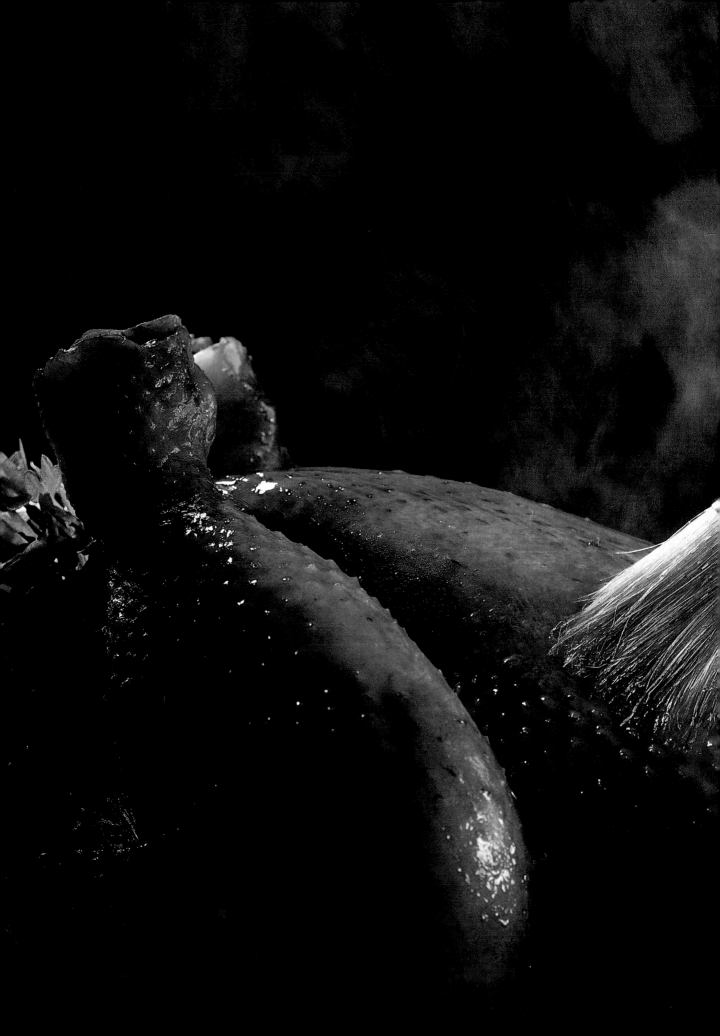

POULTRY
AND GAME

Chicken and turkey are ever
popular at the table and need
never be predictable. Exploit
their versatility and make
simple burgers or sweet and
sour apricot chicken, homely
stews or exotic dishes from other
continents. Poultry gives you
meat as high in protein as red
meat but lower in fat – if you
remember to take off the skin.
Game, too, can be low in fat,
so there are tempting recipes for
dainty quail, plump pigeons
and full-flavoured venison.

Roast chicken with a stuffing of figs, rice and thyme

SERVES 6
PREPARATION TIME: 50 minutes
COOKING TIME: 1 hour 30 minutes
OVEN: Preheat to 200°C (400°F, gas mark 6)

For the stuffing:
1 large onion, peeled and finely chopped
1 clove garlic, peeled and crushed
1 carrot, peeled and finely diced
3 level teaspoons chopped fresh thyme leaves,
or 1 level teaspoon dried thyme
4 level tablespoons chopped fresh parsley
Finely grated rind and juice of 1 lemon
5oz (150g) long-grain brown rice
6oz (175g) dried figs, roughly chopped
1½ pints (850ml) chicken stock
Freshly ground black pepper

4lb (1.8kg) oven-ready chicken, rinsed and well
dried with kitchen paper
2 tablespoons water
Sprig of fresh thyme
Thinly pared rind of half a lemon
2 fresh figs, sprigs of thyme and parsley
to garnish

1 To prepare the stuffing, put the onion, garlic, carrot, chopped or dried thyme, parsley, grated lemon rind, rice and figs into a large saucepan and pour in 1¼ pints (725ml) of the stock. Bring to the boil, then reduce the heat, cover and simmer for 35-40 minutes, or until the rice has absorbed all the stock. Remove from the heat, stir in the lemon juice and season with pepper.

2 Spoon about two-thirds of the rice mixture loosely inside the chicken. Do not overfill or the chicken will not cook thoroughly. Put the remainder of the stuffing into an ovenproof serving dish and stir in the remaining chicken stock. Put on the lid, or cover with foil, and set aside.

3 Place the chicken on a rack in a small roasting tin and tie its legs together with clean string. Put the water, the sprig of thyme and the thinly pared lemon rind into the tin. Roast the chicken in the heated oven for about 1 hour 30 minutes, until there is no trace of pink in the juice that seeps out when you push a fork into the thickest part of the thigh. During cooking, baste the chicken frequently with the juices that collect in the roasting tin. Put the reserved stuffing into the oven for the last 30 minutes of cooking to heat thoroughly.

4 Lift the cooked chicken onto a warmed serving plate. Cover it loosely with foil and leave to rest for 10 minutes. Skim all the fat from the roasting tin, then reheat the cooking juices and strain through a sieve into a warmed serving jug. Garnish the chicken with wedges of fresh fig and the sprigs of thyme and parsley just before serving.

Carve the chicken at the table, giving each diner some breast meat and leg meat and stuffing from inside the bird. Leave the diners to remove the chicken skin themselves. Hand round the sauce and extra stuffing separately and serve with a crisp green salad and some hot crusty rolls.

TIP
Use a potato peeler to pare off the lemon rind very thinly. It is easier to pare half the rind from a whole lemon than to grasp and pare a cut lemon.

An unusual stuffing of sweet, moist figs, seasoned with aromatic thyme, makes traditional roast chicken a dish for a special occasion. The cooking juices are absorbed into the rice and dried fruit. Roasting with the skin on keeps the chicken moist and brings out its fullest flavour, but take off the skin as you eat or the dish's fat content will be much higher.

Fricasseed chicken with onions

ONE SERVING	
CALORIES	225
TOTAL FAT	9g
SATURATED FAT	3g
CARBOHYDRATES	13g
ADDED SUGAR	0
FIBRE	3g
SODIUM	110mg

SERVES 4
PREPARATION TIME: 20 minutes
COOKING TIME: 50 minutes

2 tablespoons olive oil
4 chicken legs, each about 8oz (225g), skinned and divided into thighs and drumsticks
8 small onions, peeled
4 cloves garlic, peeled and crushed

8fl oz (225ml) chicken stock
2 tablespoons whisky
½ level teaspoon dried tarragon
2 medium carrots, peeled and sliced diagonally
6oz (175g) button mushrooms, wiped and quartered
2 teaspoons lemon juice
Freshly ground black pepper
4oz (115g) low-fat natural yoghurt

TIP
When skinning the chicken pieces, slit the skin with kitchen shears then grip one end of it with a piece of kitchen paper and pull firmly away from you.

This tender dish, using the darker meat from a chicken, has its creamy sauce laced with a dash of whisky.

1 Heat half the oil in a large frying pan and cook the chicken pieces in it over a moderate heat for 7-8 minutes, turning them to brown all over. Lift them from the pan and set aside.

2 Cook the onions and garlic gently in the pan for 8-10 minutes, until soft. Stir in the stock, whisky and tarragon. Return the chicken to the pan and bring the sauce to the boil. Lower the heat, cover and simmer for 25 minutes.

3 Heat the remaining oil in a heavy-based saucepan and cook the carrots and mushrooms

in it over a moderately high heat, uncovered, for 4-5 minutes, stirring frequently.

4 Add the carrots, mushrooms and lemon juice to the chicken, season with pepper, cover and cook gently for 5 minutes. Lift the chicken into a heated serving dish with a slotted spoon.

5 Stir the yoghurt into the sauce and heat without boiling, then pour over the chicken.

Serve with red cabbage, rice and parsley sprigs. Dry sherry or wine can replace the whisky.

Gardener's chicken

SERVES 4
PREPARATION TIME: 25 minutes
COOKING TIME: 1 hour 15 minutes
OVEN: Preheat to 200°C (400°F, gas mark 6)

ONE SERVING	
CALORIES	290
TOTAL FAT	6g
SATURATED FAT	2g
CARBOHYDRATES	28g
ADDED SUGAR	0
FIBRE	7g
SODIUM	130mg

Vegetables are the main focus of this dish. Cooked in the roasting tin with the chicken, they absorb the delicious juices from the meat as well as the flavours of the stock and wine.

16 small new potatoes, scrubbed
2 medium onions, peeled and quartered
4 medium carrots, peeled and cut into strips
1 medium parsnip, peeled and cut into finger-length strips
2 small leeks, trimmed, cut into rings and well washed
4 chicken legs, each about 8oz (225g), divided into thighs and drumsticks
¾ pint (425ml) chicken stock
4fl oz (115ml) dry white wine
1 tablespoon lemon juice
3 cloves garlic, peeled and finely chopped
1 level teaspoon dried oregano
½ level teaspoon dried thyme
Freshly ground black pepper
4oz (115g) fresh or frozen peas
2 level tablespoons chopped fresh parsley

1 Mix the potatoes, onions, carrots, parsnip and leeks in a small roasting tin and lay the chicken pieces on top.

2 Pour the stock, wine and lemon juice over the chicken. Sprinkle with the garlic, oregano and thyme and season with pepper.

3 Cook, uncovered, for 1 hour 15 minutes, or until no pink juices ooze from the chicken thighs when pricked. During cooking, turn the chicken and stir the vegetables occasionally, and baste with the pan juices. Add the peas for the last 10 minutes of cooking. If the juices evaporate too quickly pour in a little water.

4 Put the chicken, vegetables and juices on a warm serving dish and sprinkle with parsley.

Give each diner a thigh and a drumstick and leave them to remove the skin themselves. A fresh green salad contrasts well with the succulent baked vegetables.

Chicken and mushroom hotpot

SERVES 6
PREPARATION TIME: 30 minutes
COOKING TIME: 1 hour 15 minutes
OVEN: Preheat to 200°C (400°F, gas mark 6)

2 tablespoons olive oil
4 boneless chicken breasts, each about 5oz (150g),
skinned and cut into cubes
1 medium onion, peeled and chopped
2 sticks celery, trimmed and chopped
2 cloves garlic, peeled and crushed
6oz (175g) button mushrooms, wiped and halved
2 level teaspoons peeled and grated root ginger,
or ¼ level teaspoon ground ginger

2 sprigs fresh parsley or thyme
2 level tablespoons plain flour
¼ pint (150ml) dry white wine
½ pint (285ml) chicken stock
Freshly ground black pepper
1lb (450g) potatoes, peeled and thinly sliced

1 Heat the oil in a large, nonstick saucepan
and fry the chicken in it over a high heat for
2-3 minutes, turning the cubes to brown all
over. Put the chicken on a plate and set aside.

2 Brown the onion, celery and garlic in the
pan over a moderate heat for 5 minutes. Stir in
the mushrooms, ginger and one sprig of parsley
or thyme, and cook for 3 minutes. Mix in the
flour then, little by little, the wine and stock;
bring to the boil, stirring. Season with pepper,
add the chicken and cook for 5 minutes.

3 Pour the chicken into an ovenproof dish and
cover with potato slices, seasoning with pepper.

4 Cover the dish with foil and cook in the
heated oven for 1 hour. Take off the foil and
cook for a further 15-20 minutes, until the
potatoes are tender and golden brown on top.

Serve the hotpot right away, garnished with the
remaining parsley or thyme and accompanied
by strips of carrot and courgette, steamed but
still slightly firm.

*The crisp potato topping absorbs flavours from the
aromatic sauce to create a warming winter dish.*

Chicken with onion and herb stuffing

SERVES 6
PREPARATION TIME: 20 minutes
COOKING TIME: 1 hour 35 minutes
OVEN: Preheat to 230°C (450°F, gas mark 8)

4½ -5lb (2-2.3kg) oven-ready chicken
1 level tablespoon fresh thyme leaves,
or 1 level teaspoon dried thyme

4 level tablespoons each chopped fresh basil and
parsley, or 1 level tablespoon each dried basil
and parsley
6 spring onions, trimmed and finely chopped
Freshly ground black pepper
1 tablespoon olive oil
1 large onion, peeled and finely chopped
1 stick celery, trimmed and finely chopped

3 cloves garlic, peeled and crushed
1lb (450g) ripe tomatoes, skinned, de-seeded
and chopped
¼ pint (150ml) dry white wine
1 bay leaf
½ level teaspoon fennel seeds, crushed
Thyme sprigs to garnish

1 Rinse the chicken under the cold tap and pat it dry with kitchen paper. Carefully loosen the skin from the breast on each side of the chicken by easing your fingertips under the skin from the neck end.

2 Mix half the thyme with the basil, parsley and spring onions, and season with pepper. Spread the stuffing evenly on the chicken breast under the skin, then tuck the neck flap under the chicken and secure it with a skewer.

3 Put the chicken in a roasting tin and cook for 20-30 minutes in the heated oven, until it is very lightly browned.

4 Meanwhile, heat the oil in a flameproof casserole and cook the onion, celery and garlic in it over a moderate heat, stirring frequently, for about 5 minutes. Stir in the tomatoes, bring to the boil then reduce to a simmer.

5 Lower the oven temperature to 200°C (400°F, gas mark 6). Lift the chicken into the casserole. Pour off the fat from the roasting tin, reserving the juices. Pour the wine into the roasting tin and set it over a direct heat, stirring with a wooden spoon to loosen the browned bits as it comes to the boil. Pour the juices over the chicken in the casserole.

6 Add the bay leaf, fennel seeds and the remaining half of the thyme and season with pepper. When the casserole returns to the boil, put on the lid and cook in the heated oven for about 1 hour.

7 Lift the chicken onto a warmed serving dish, garnish it with sprigs of thyme and keep hot. Remove the fat from the sauce, discard the bay

leaf and blend half the sauce in a food processor for 5-10 seconds. Stir this back into the casserole. Spoon some of the sauce over the chicken and serve the rest separately.

Carve the chicken at the table, leaving the diners to remove the skin for themselves. Lightly cooked cabbage and roast potatoes would complete a hearty dish.

> **TIP**
> *Draw pieces of kitchen paper across the sauce in the casserole to absorb the fat that has risen to the top.*

Cooking the chicken in a covered casserole keeps it beautifully moist and lets it take in the fragrance of the herbs and wine, and at the same time add its own rich taste to the tomato sauce.

The spicy marinade permeating this chicken re-creates the authentic flavour of a classic Indian dish, which is traditionally cooked in a tandoor, a clay oven, over a charcoal fire.

Tandoori chicken

SERVES 4
PREPARATION TIME: 15 minutes, plus at least 4 hours to marinate
COOKING TIME: 30 minutes
OVEN: Preheat to 180°C (350°F, gas mark 4)

4oz (115g) Greek yoghurt
1 small onion, peeled and very finely chopped
1 level tablespoon peeled and grated root ginger, or ¹/₂ level teaspoon ground ginger
2 cloves garlic, peeled and crushed
1 tablespoon lime juice
1¹/₂ level teaspoons ground coriander
1 level teaspoon each ground cumin, ground cardamom and turmeric
¹/₄ level teaspoon cayenne pepper
1 level tablespoon paprika
4 chicken breast and wing portions, each about 8oz (225g), skinned
Lime wedges and parsley to garnish

1 Blend the yoghurt, onion, ginger, garlic and lime juice in a food processor for 30 seconds, or combine them with a rotary hand whisk. Mix in the coriander, cumin, cardamom, turmeric, cayenne pepper and paprika. Pour into a large, glass or china dish, put in the chicken pieces and turn to coat with the yoghurt mixture. Cover and refrigerate for at least 4 hours or up to 24 hours, turning to recoat occasionally.

2 Heat the grill, arrange the chicken on the grill rack and cook under a moderate heat for 8 minutes on each side, until browned.

3 Put the chicken pieces in a nonstick baking tin and cook in the heated oven for about 15 minutes or until the juices run clear when the chicken is pierced with a sharp knife.

4 Lift the chicken onto a warm serving plate and garnish with the lime wedges and parsley.

The traditional accompaniment for the hot, sharp taste of tandoori chicken cannot be bettered so serve it with basmati rice perhaps sprinkled with some chopped peppers. A mixed salad makes a cooling side dish.

ONE SERVING

CALORIES 190

TOTAL FAT 7g

SATURATED FAT 3g

CARBOHYDRATES 2g

ADDED SUGAR 0

FIBRE 1g

SODIUM 110mg

Chicken and vegetable stew

SERVES 4
PREPARATION TIME: 30 minutes
COOKING TIME: 1 hour 35 minutes

3lb (1.4kg) oven-ready chicken
5 large sprigs of parsley
6 black peppercorns
1 bay leaf
1¼ pints (725ml) chicken stock
1½ level teaspoons each mixed dried herbs
and dried sage
4 small turnips, peeled and quartered
2 large sticks celery, trimmed and chopped
2 medium potatoes, peeled and thickly sliced
14oz (400g) tinned peeled tomatoes
1 medium onion, peeled and chopped
4oz (115g) fresh or frozen sweetcorn kernels
4oz (115g) runner beans, trimmed and sliced
Freshly ground black pepper

1 Rinse the chicken under the cold tap and
put it in a large saucepan. Tie the parsley,
peppercorns and bay leaf in a small square of
muslin or clean linen and put into the saucepan
with the stock and ½ teaspoon each
of the mixed herbs and sage.

2 Bring to the boil, then reduce the heat
and simmer, covered, for 1 hour or until the
chicken falls easily off the bone. Lift the
chicken onto a heated plate.

3 Skim all the fat off the stock and put in the
turnips, celery, potatoes, tomatoes, onion and
another ½ teaspoon of mixed herbs and sage.
Bring back to the boil, then cover and simmer
gently for 20 minutes.

4 Take the skin off the chicken and lift
the meat off the bones. Cut it into chunks
and return to the saucepan together with the
sweetcorn and runner beans. Continue to
simmer, covered, for 15 minutes, stirring
occasionally. Take out the wrapped herbs, and
season the stew with pepper and the
remaining mixed herbs and sage.

*The original version of this dish, created by
American Indians, had rabbit and squirrel in it
instead of chicken. The stew develops a fuller flavour
if it is cooked the day before you need it.*

ONE SERVING	
CALORIES	280
TOTAL FAT	7g
SATURATED FAT	2g
CARBOHYDRATES	11g
ADDED SUGAR	0
FIBRE	4g
SODIUM	185mg

The thick skin keeps the duckling moist during cooking, but should not be eaten. It is high in fat and would increase the calorie count.

Roast duckling with lime sauce

ONE SERVING	
CALORIES	205
TOTAL FAT	7g
SATURATED FAT	2g
CARBOHYDRATES	6g
ADDED SUGAR	4g
FIBRE	0
SODIUM	165mg

SERVES 4
PREPARATION: 15 minutes
COOKING TIME: 1 hour 45 minutes
OVEN: Preheat to 230°C (450°F, gas mark 8)

4½ - 5lb (2-2.3kg) oven-ready duckling
Freshly ground black pepper
1 small onion, peeled
1 small cooking apple, peeled and halved
2 limes, gently scrubbed, rind thinly peeled and finely shredded, juice strained
1 level tablespoon granulated sugar
½ pint (285ml) chicken stock
Slices of lime to garnish

1 Rinse the duckling, wipe it inside and out with kitchen paper and season it with pepper. Push the onion and apple inside the duckling and prick its skin all over with a fork. Place the bird on a rack in a roasting tin and cook in the heated oven for 45 minutes. Turn down the heat to 200°C (400°F, gas mark 6) and cook for a further 45 minutes, basting the duckling from time to time with the cooking juices. Lift the duckling onto a heated plate lined with kitchen paper to drain, and keep hot.

2 Blanch the lime rind in boiling water for 2-3 minutes, then drain and put the shreds to one side.

3 Pour off and discard the fat from the roasting tin. Scrape the remaining cooking juices from the bottom of the tin into a small saucepan. Heat the juices gently with the lime juice and sugar for 1-2 minutes. Mix in the chicken stock, bring to the boil, and boil the sauce hard for 8-10 minutes, until reduced to about a cupful. Stir in the shreds of lime rind and keep hot.

4 Carve the duckling, placing some breast slices and a thigh or leg piece on each diner's heated plate. Leave the diners to remove the skin for themselves. Trickle 2 tablespoons of sauce round each serving and garnish with the lime slices.

When Seville oranges are in season you can use them instead of limes for an equally strong, sharp sauce. The duck is very rich, so serve steamed potatoes with it and have a fresh-tasting celeriac salad on the side.

Duck satay

ONE SERVING

CALORIES 230

TOTAL FAT 12g

SATURATED FAT 3g

CARBOHYDRATES 6g

ADDED SUGAR 0

FIBRE 0

SODIUM 360mg

TIP
If you are using wooden skewers, soak them in cold water for 15-20 minutes before threading the meat on them. This helps to prevent them from scorching.

SERVES 4
PREPARATION TIME: 10 minutes, plus 2 hours to marinate
COOKING TIME: 10 minutes
OVEN: Preheat to 200°C (400°F, gas mark 6)

½ level teaspoon ground ginger
1 tablespoon soy sauce
1 teaspoon Worcestershire sauce
Finely grated rind and juice of 2 oranges
Freshly ground black pepper
1lb (450g) duck breast, without skin or bone, cubed
4 long wooden or metal skewers
2oz (60g) unsalted cashew nuts
Orange wedges, strips of rind and parsley to garnish

1 Mix the ginger, soy sauce, Worcestershire sauce and orange rind and juice in a glass or china casserole, and season with pepper. Stir in the duck, cover and refrigerate for 2 hours.

2 Thread the duck onto the skewers. Put them in a roasting tin, spoon on the marinade and cook in the heated oven for about 10 minutes, or until the duck is cooked through and tender.

3 Meanwhile spread the cashew nuts on a baking tray and roast in the oven for 5 minutes, until golden brown. Set aside.

4 When the duck is cooked, lift the skewers onto a heated serving dish, cover and keep hot.

5 Put the cashew nuts into a food processor with the cooking juices from the duck and blend until smooth. Reheat, put into a warmed serving bowl and top with strips of orange rind.

Serve the duck satay with rice and garnish with orange wedges and parsley. Stir-fried mangetout make a crisp accompaniment.

In this adaptation of a traditional South-east Asian dish, the marinaded and skewered meat is roasted and its juices are added to the spicy nut sauce.

Turkey escalopes with sherry sauce

SERVES 4
PREPARATION TIME: 10 minutes
COOKING TIME: 10 minutes

ONE SERVING	
CALORIES	235
TOTAL FAT	10g
SATURATED FAT	3g
CARBOHYDRATES	7g
ADDED SUGAR	0
FIBRE	0
SODIUM	130mg

3 level tablespoons plain flour
½ level teaspoon dried rosemary
½ level teaspoon dried thyme
Freshly ground black pepper
4 turkey breast escalopes, each about 4oz (115g),
beaten out thin
2 tablespoons olive oil

4 tablespoons dry sherry
6 tablespoons chicken stock
½ level teaspoon cornflour
4oz (115g) Greek yoghurt
1 level teaspoon Dijon mustard

1 Mix together the flour, rosemary, thyme and pepper. Coat each turkey escalope with the seasoned flour and shake off any excess.

2 Heat the oil in a nonstick frying pan and cook the escalopes in it over a moderate heat for 2-3 minutes on each side, until golden brown and cooked through. Lift them onto kitchen paper for a moment to drain, and then onto a heated serving dish. Keep hot.

3 Skim off any oil from the frying pan, stir the sherry into the browned juices in the pan and simmer for 30 seconds. Blend the stock with the cornflour and pour into the pan. Stir until it comes to the boil, then add the yoghurt and mustard. Stir over a low heat without boiling for 2-3 minutes, until the sauce is slightly thickened. Spoon the sauce over the turkey.

A mixture of white and wild rice is a good foil for the turkey in its rich sauce. Serve a leafy side-salad for a crisp and colourful contrast.

Quick and easy to prepare, the lavish sauce of sherry, Greek yoghurt and mustard transforms a simple dish into a succulent feast fit for any occasion.

Turkey with sweet potato stuffing

SERVES 8
PREPARATION TIME: 45 minutes
COOKING TIME: 1 hour 30 minutes
OVEN: Preheat to 230°C (450°F, gas mark 8)

ONE SERVING	
CALORIES	300
TOTAL FAT	5g
SATURATED FAT	1g
CARBOHYDRATES	23g
ADDED SUGAR	0
FIBRE	3g
SODIUM	110mg

1½ lb (680g) orange-fleshed sweet potatoes,
peeled and cut into small pieces
2 tablespoons olive oil
1 medium carrot, peeled and chopped
1 medium onion, peeled and chopped

1 stick celery, trimmed and chopped
1 small leek, washed and chopped
8 leaves fresh sage, chopped
Grated rind and juice of 1 large orange
1 turkey crown (double breast), about 5lb (2.3kg),
in one piece on the bone and with skin on
Skewers or clean, thin string to secure
3 level tablespoons plain flour
1 pint (570ml) turkey or chicken stock
Orange wedges and sage sprigs to garnish

1 Cook the sweet potatoes in unsalted boiling water for about 15 minutes, until they feel tender when pierced with a knife.

2 Meanwhile heat half the oil in a heavy-based saucepan and cook the carrot, onion, celery and leek in it over a moderate heat for 10 minutes, stirring frequently. Mix in the sage and cook for 1 minute.

3 Drain and mash the sweet potato, beat in the orange rind and stir in the vegetable and sage mixture. Leave this stuffing to cool.

4 Loosen the skin round the neck end of the turkey by pushing your fingers between the flesh and the skin. Spoon the stuffing in under the skin and secure with skewers or by sewing with a large darning needle and string.

5 Rub the remaining oil round a roasting tin, lay the turkey in it and roast in the heated oven for 30 minutes. Lower the temperature to 190°C (375°F, gas mark 5), pour the orange juice over the turkey and cook for 45 minutes longer, basting occasionally. If the turkey skin browns too quickly, cover loosely with foil.

6 When the turkey feels tender and there is no trace of pink in the juice that oozes out when you push a fork into the thickest part of the meat, lift it onto a heated serving dish. Cover with foil and leave to rest.

7 Skim any fat from the juices remaining in the roasting tin. Blend the flour into the juices and gradually stir in the stock. Bring to the boil, stirring continuously, then simmer for 5 minutes. Pour into a warmed serving jug.

Remove the skewers or string from the turkey. Carve the meat and serve it with the stuffing and a garnish of orange wedges and sage sprigs. Hand round the gravy separately. Brussels sprouts offset the sweetness of the dish. If sweet potatoes are unobtainable you can use ordinary potatoes but the taste will be less rich.

The zest of fresh orange permeates the chestnut flavour of sweet potato in this stuffing. The combination is popular in the United States, where it is a traditional accompaniment to turkey and often forms part of November's annual Thanksgiving feast.

Pheasant casserole with apple and cabbage

SERVES 4
PREPARATION TIME: 35 minutes
COOKING TIME: 1 hour
OVEN: Preheat to 180°C (350°F, gas mark 4)

2 tablespoons olive oil
2 oven-ready pheasants, each about 1¼ lb (550g),
cut in half and any lead shot removed
4 shallots, or 1 medium onion, peeled and sliced

8oz (225g) white cabbage, finely sliced
8oz (225g) red cabbage, finely sliced
1lb (450g) potatoes, peeled and chopped
2 level teaspoons paprika
6 juniper berries, crushed
About ¼ pint (150ml) dry red wine
1lb (450g) cooking apples, peeled, cored and cut
into thick slices
Freshly ground black pepper

ONE SERVING	
CALORIES 510	
TOTAL FAT 20g	
SATURATED FAT 5g	
CARBOHYDRATES 34g	
ADDED SUGAR 0	
FIBRE 5g	
SODIUM 180mg	

Older pheasants can be used for this dish, since casseroling with wine and apple makes them meltingly tender.

1 Heat the oil in a large, flameproof casserole and brown the pheasants in it on all sides over a fairly high heat. Lift the pheasants onto a plate.

2 Cook the shallots or onion in the casserole for 1-2 minutes. Mix in all the cabbage, the potatoes, paprika and juniper berries and pour on the wine. Cover and cook for 5 minutes.

3 Add the apple slices and season with pepper. Lay the pheasant halves on top, pouring over any juices from the plate. Cover and cook in the

heated oven for about 1 hour, or until the meat feels tender and there is no pink in the juice that seeps out when you push a fork into the thickest part of the thigh. Check from time to time that there is some liquid in the casserole and add a little more wine if necessary.

Give each diner some vegetables, apple and sauce with their meat. Leave the diners to remove the skin from their pheasant. The dish is complete as it is but offer some rolls for mopping up the delicious sauce.

TIP
If the lid of your casserole does not fit very tightly, cover the dish with foil, crimped round the rim to fit snugly. The cabbage will burn on the base and spoil the flavour if all the liquid evaporates.

Roast pheasant with prunes

SERVES 4
PREPARATION TIME: 30 minutes
COOKING TIME: 1 hour
OVEN: Preheat to 220°C (425°F, gas mark 7)

2 oven-ready pheasants, each about 1½ lb (680g)
8-16 crushed juniper berries (to taste)
1 tablespoon fresh rosemary leaves,
or 1 level teaspoon dried rosemary, crumbled
1 tablespoon olive oil
4 bay leaves
16 ready-to-use stoned prunes
2 rashers unsmoked back bacon, fat removed
Wooden cocktail sticks
¼ pint (150ml) water
2 level teaspoons plain flour
¼ pint (150ml) chicken stock
1 level tablespoon redcurrant jelly
Sprigs of rosemary to garnish

1 Remove any feather tips and lead shot from the birds, then rinse them out and wipe them inside and out with kitchen paper.

2 Mix the juniper berries and rosemary leaves with the oil and spread inside the pheasants. Push a bay leaf and 8 prunes inside each bird. Lay a bay leaf and a rasher of bacon across the breast of each bird and fix with cocktail sticks.

3 Put the pheasants in a roasting tin and add the water to keep them moist. Cook for 1 hour in the heated oven until browned and tender, basting occasionally.

4 Lift the pheasants onto a warmed meat plate, cover and leave to rest.

5 Stir the flour into the cooking juices and gradually mix in the stock. Bring to the boil, to work in the hardened juices from the bottom of the tin. Stir in the redcurrant jelly and any juices from the meat plate. Lower the heat and simmer for 3-4 minutes until slightly thickened. Strain into a warmed serving jug.

Rosemary and juniper berries inside the pheasants give the meat a savoury bitterness with a hint of gin, which is sweetened by the juicy prunes.

Remove the cocktail sticks, bacon and bay leaves and give each diner some slices of breast and a leg, some of the prunes and a spoonful or two of sauce; hand round the rest of the sauce separately. Garnish with the rosemary and leave the diners to remove the pheasant skin for themselves. A purée of root vegetables and roast potatoes are well-flavoured enough to match the robust taste of the pheasant.

ONE SERVING	
CALORIES	510
TOTAL FAT	20g
SATURATED FAT	6g
CARBOHYDRATES	24g
ADDED SUGAR	3g
FIBRE	3g
SODIUM	405mg

Pigeons braised with orange and rice

SERVES 4
PREPARATION TIME: 20 minutes
COOKING TIME: 1 hour 30 minutes
OVEN: Preheat to 160°C (325°F, gas mark 3)

1 tablespoon olive oil
4 shallots, or 1 medium onion, peeled and chopped
1 clove garlic, peeled and crushed
4 oven-ready pigeons
About ½ pint (285ml) vegetable stock
¼ pint (150ml) fresh orange juice
6oz (175g) long-grain rice
2 large carrots, peeled and diced
8oz (225g) tinned peeled water chestnuts in water,
drained and diced
1 level tablespoon coarsely chopped fresh parsley
⅛ level teaspoon salt
Freshly ground black pepper
1 large orange, peel and pith removed
2oz (60g) toasted pine nuts
Watercress sprigs to garnish

1 Heat the oil in a large, flameproof casserole
and cook the shallots or onion and the garlic
in it over a high heat for 1-2 minutes, stirring
frequently, until lightly browned.

2 Put the pigeons in the casserole and brown
them well on all sides. Lower the heat and pour
in the stock and orange juice. Cover and cook
in the heated oven for 45 minutes.

3 Stir the rice, carrots, water chestnuts and
parsley into the casserole and season with the
salt and pepper. Cover again and return to the
oven for another 45 minutes. Stir the rice
from time to time and add a little more stock
or water if the casserole is becoming dry.

4 Using a small sharp knife, cut down the
sides of the orange segments to free them from
their membranes. When the rice is cooked all
through and the pigeons are tender, spoon the
rice mixture onto a warm serving dish and
sprinkle with the pine nuts. Arrange the
pigeons on top. Garnish with the orange
segments and watercress.

ONE SERVING	
CALORIES	630
TOTAL FAT	29g
SATURATED FAT	6g
CARBOHYDRATES	58g
ADDED SUGAR	0
FIBRE	4g
SODIUM	205mg

TIP
*To toast the pine
nuts, spread them
on foil and grill
under a medium
heat for 1-2
minutes. Stir
frequently to toast
evenly as the nuts
burn quickly.*

Braising brings out the full flavour of the rich, dark pigeon meat, which is enhanced by the tartness of oranges and absorbed by the rice.

Braised quail make an attractive dish for a special occasion. These little game birds should not be hung, but enjoyed as fresh as possible.

Braised quail with mushrooms

SERVES 4
PREPARATION TIME: 30 minutes
COOKING TIME: 40 minutes
OVEN: Preheat to 180°C (350°F, gas mark 4)

1 tablespoon olive oil
8 oven-ready quail
1 small onion, peeled and finely chopped
2 rashers unsmoked back bacon, trimmed of fat and finely chopped
1 level tablespoon plain flour
¾ pint (425ml) chicken stock
2oz (60g) pearl barley
1 large carrot, peeled and diced
4oz (115g) button mushrooms, wiped and finely chopped
1 teaspoon lemon juice
3 level tablespoons chopped fresh parsley
Freshly ground black pepper

1 Heat the oil in a large, flameproof casserole and cook the quail in it over a high heat for about 5 minutes, turning them to brown all over. Remove from casserole and set aside.

2 Fry the onion and bacon gently in the casserole for 2 minutes. Stir in the flour and then the stock, pearl barley and carrot. Bring to the boil, stirring continuously.

3 Add the mushrooms, lemon juice and 1 tablespoon of the parsley, and season with pepper. Return the quail to the casserole, bring to the boil, cover and cook in the heated oven for about 40 minutes, or until the quail are tender. Sprinkle with the remaining parsley.

Sautéed brussels sprouts and potato slices blend well with the quail. Leave the diners to remove the skin from their quail and remind them to watch out for the small bones.

Calabrian rabbit

TIP

For meat similar to well-flavoured free-range chicken, choose farmed rabbit. For a fuller and more gamey flavour, try to get a wild rabbit.

Cooking rabbit in this way keeps it succulent. Like all lean meats with no fat to moisten them, it is best cooked with plenty of liquid. The sweet thyme gives its aroma to the meat.

SERVES 4
PREPARATION TIME: 20 minutes
COOKING TIME: 1 hour 15 minutes
OVEN: Preheat to 180°C (350°F, gas mark 4)

1 tablespoon olive oil
8 even-sized rabbit joints, about 1¾ lb (800g) together
1 level tablespoon plain flour
1 pint (570ml) chicken stock
12 small new potatoes, 8oz (225g) together, washed
12 small onions, about 6oz (175g) together, peeled
Thinly pared rind and juice of 1 lemon
½ oz (15g) fresh thyme sprigs
Freshly ground black pepper

1 Heat the oil in a large, flameproof casserole and brown the rabbit pieces in it over a high heat for about 5 minutes. Stir in the flour and then the stock. Add the potatoes, onions and lemon rind and juice. Set aside 4 thyme sprigs and put the rest in the casserole. Season with pepper and bring to the boil.

2 Cover and cook in the heated oven for 1 hour, or until the meat is ready to drop off the bones. Garnish with the reserved sprigs of fresh thyme.

Grilled rabbit

SERVES 4
PREPARATION: 10 minutes, plus at least 6 hours
to marinate
COOKING TIME: 15 minutes

1½ lb (680g) farmed rabbit, divided into
even-sized joints
2 level tablespoons soured cream
Freshly ground black pepper

1 tablespoon lemon juice
Curly endive, lemon slices and flat-leaf parsley
to garnish

1 Lay the rabbit joints in one layer in a dish.
Season the cream well with pepper and coat
the rabbit pieces evenly with it. Cover with a lid
and refrigerate for at least 6 hours, and up to
24 hours if more convenient.

2 Thirty minutes before cooking, remove the
rabbit from the refrigerator, uncover and leave
at room temperature.

3 Arrange the rabbit joints on the grill rack
and cook under a hot grill for about 7 minutes
on each side, or until cooked through and
golden brown.

4 Lift the rabbit joints onto a heated serving
dish and sprinkle the lemon juice over them.
Garnish with the endive, lemon slices and
parsley, and serve immediately.

Steamed new carrots and warm herb rolls go
well with this simple, quickly cooked dish.

*The success of this dish depends on the tenderness
of the meat, which is assured if you allow it ample
time to marinate in the soured cream.*

Rabbit pie

SERVES 4
PREPARATION TIME: 30 minutes
COOKING TIME: 1 hour 10 minutes
OVEN: Preheat to 200°C (400°F, gas mark 6)

2 tablespoons olive oil
2 medium onions, peeled and sliced
1 clove garlic, peeled and crushed
2oz (60g) unsmoked back bacon with fat
removed, chopped
1½ lb (680g) boneless rabbit portions cut into cubes
2 level tablespoons plain flour

1 pint (570ml) chicken stock
Sprig fresh thyme
Sprig fresh parsley
4oz (115g) ready-to-use stoned prunes
Freshly ground black pepper
3 filo pastry sheets, 20×12in (51×30cm)

1 Heat half the oil in a large frying pan and
cook the onion, garlic and bacon in it over a
moderate heat for 5 minutes, stirring
frequently. Spoon into an ovenproof dish,
using a slotted spoon.

TIP
Unpack the filo sheets only when you are ready to use them and cover with a clean, damp cloth to prevent them from becoming brittle.

2 Toss the rabbit in 1 tablespoon of the flour, shake off the excess and fry in the oil left in the pan until golden brown all over. Spoon the meat into the dish.

3 Stir the remaining flour into the pan juices and cook for 1 minute. Gradually stir in the stock and bring to the boil, stirring continuously, then add the thyme, parsley and prunes and season with pepper.

4 Pour the sauce over the rabbit and stir well. Cover with a lid or foil and cook in the heated oven for 1 hour.

5 When the rabbit is tender, quickly brush the filo pastry with the remaining oil and cut each sheet into 15 squares. Cut the squares in half diagonally to make triangles. Take the cover off the dish and arrange overlapping filo triangles over the pie filling.

6 Return the dish to the oven and cook for a further 5-10 minutes, until the pastry is crisp and golden brown.

Mashed swede or crisp curly kale, with their slightly peppery tastes, go well with the robust flavours of the pie.

The crisp filo pastry gives a light, elegant finish to an otherwise hearty pie that allies the savoury rabbit meat with dark, plump prunes.

These thick, pink slices of venison have been kept moist during cooking by the wrapping of cabbage leaves and a layer of redcurrant jelly.

Roast venison parcel

SERVES 6
PREPARATION TIME: 20 minutes
COOKING TIME: 40 minutes, plus 15 minutes to rest
OVEN: Preheat to 200°C (400°F, gas mark 6)

1 tablespoon olive oil
1 1/2 lb (680g) prime boneless venison joint
1/8 level teaspoon salt
Freshly ground black pepper
6-7 large green cabbage leaves
1 level tablespoon redcurrant jelly
2 level teaspoons fresh thyme leaves
Watercress to garnish

1 Rub the oil over the venison and season it with the salt and pepper.

2 Blanch the cabbage in unsalted boiling water for 2 minutes. Rinse with cold water, dry on kitchen paper and trim out the thick stalks.

3 Heat a nonstick frying pan over a high heat and dry-fry the meat in it quickly, turning until it is brown all over. Remove from the heat and leave until cooled enough to touch.

4 Snip off any string from the meat and trim off any fat. Spread the redcurrant jelly over the meat and sprinkle with thyme leaves. Cover the venison completely with the cabbage leaves, then wrap it in nonstick baking paper.

5 Put the parcel of venison in a roasting tin and cook in the heated oven for 40 minutes. Remove from the oven and leave to rest for 15 minutes before unwrapping.

Carve the meat into very thick slices; it will be cooked but still slightly pink. Garnish with the watercress and serve with braised leeks and sesame potatoes.

Venison stew

ONE SERVING

CALORIES 320

TOTAL FAT 14g

SATURATED FAT 4g

CARBOHYDRATES 5g

ADDED SUGAR 0

FIBRE 1g

SODIUM 120mg

Lean, richly flavoured venison gives a luxury lift to this winter stew. Use saddle of venison when you can, to make the most tender dish.

SERVES 6
PREPARATION TIME: 20 minutes
COOKING TIME: 1 hour

2 tablespoons olive oil
1½ lb (680g) venison cubes, trimmed of fat
2 carrots, peeled and diced
2 sticks celery, trimmed and sliced
1 onion, peeled and cut into rings
1 level tablespoon plain flour
1 pint (570ml) veal stock
4 juniper berries
1 level tablespoon chopped fresh lovage or celery leaves
Freshly ground black pepper
Shredded lovage or celery leaves to garnish

1 Heat the oil in a large, heavy-based saucepan and toss the meat in it over a high heat to brown the cubes quickly. Lift out the meat into a heatproof dish, using a slotted spoon.

2 Fry the carrots, celery and onion in the same pan for 5 minutes. Stir in the flour and cook it for 2 minutes before gradually blending in the stock. Bring to the boil, stirring continuously.

3 Return the venison to the pan, stir in the juniper berries and chopped lovage or celery leaves and season with pepper. Bring back to the boil, then lower the heat, cover and simmer for 1 hour, or until the meat is very tender. Pour into a warmed serving dish and garnish with the shredded lovage or celery leaves.

Mashed potato and swede go well with the savoury broth of this dish.

BEEF, LAMB AND PORK

Red meat is invaluable for the complete protein, vitamins and minerals it contributes to the diet, but these go hand in hand with the saturated fats that should be avoided. The knack is to make a little meat go a long way, and these recipes show how to do it. They skilfully use prudent portions in delicious dishes, cooked by roasting and stewing and by quick grilling and stir-frying to cut down fat but keep flavour intact.

Sweet and sour braised beef

ONE SERVING	
CALORIES 310	
TOTAL FAT 12g	
SATURATED FAT 4g	
CARBOHYDRATES 15g	
ADDED SUGAR 3g	
FIBRE 2g	
SODIUM 220mg	

SERVES 6
PREPARATION TIME: 25 minutes, plus 24 hours
to marinate
COOKING TIME: 45 minutes
OVEN: Preheat to 160°C (325°F, gas mark 3)

2 tablespoons olive oil
4fl oz (115ml) white wine vinegar
6fl oz (175ml) dry white wine
Finely grated rind of 1 lemon
¼ level teaspoon cayenne pepper

1 large onion, peeled, halved and thinly sliced
2 bay leaves
2lb (900g) rump steak with fat removed, cut
into six pieces
1 level tablespoon demerara sugar
2 level tablespoons plain flour
1 level tablespoon tomato purée
6fl oz (175ml) beef stock
⅛ level teaspoon salt
2 medium mangoes, peeled, stoned and sliced

1 Mix half the oil with the vinegar, wine, lemon rind, cayenne pepper, onion and bay leaves in a shallow glass or china dish. Put in the steak and turn it over to coat it well with the marinade. Cover the dish and refrigerate for 24 hours, turning the meat from time to time. Lift the meat onto kitchen paper to drain. Take the onion and bay leaves out of the marinade and set aside. Strain and keep the liquid.

2 Heat the remaining oil over a gentle heat in a flameproof casserole. Sprinkle in the sugar, let it dissolve and as soon as it begins to brown, put in the pieces of steak and brown them all over. Lift the meat onto a plate and set aside.

3 Cook the onion in the casserole over a moderate heat for 1 minute, then stir in the flour and cook for 1 minute. Gradually mix in the marinade liquid, tomato purée and stock. Put back the bay leaves, add the salt and bring the sauce to the boil, stirring continuously.

4 Put the meat back in the casserole along with any juices from the plate. Stir in the mango, cover the casserole with a tightly fitting lid, or foil, and cook in the heated oven for about 45 minutes, or until the meat is tender.

Remove the bay leaves before serving. Serve the sweet and sour beef with broccoli and rice flavoured with thyme. You can use chuck steak instead of rump for a less expensive dish; increase the time in the oven to 2½ hours, adding the mango for the last hour.

Long marinating gives the beef a delicate fragrance; the marinade produces a rich, mellow sauce that is sweetened naturally with fresh mangoes.

Beef stew with tomatoes and basil

SERVES 4
PREPARATION TIME: 20 minutes
COOKING TIME: 2 hours 15 minutes

ONE SERVING
CALORIES 320
TOTAL FAT 10g
SATURATED FAT 3g
CARBOHYDRATES 24g
ADDED SUGAR 0
FIBRE 7g
SODIUM 185mg

1lb (450g) chuck steak or beef skirt with
fat removed, cut into large cubes
Freshly ground black pepper
1 tablespoon olive oil
4fl oz (115ml) red wine
14fl oz (400ml) beef stock
14oz (400g) tinned peeled tomatoes

2 sticks celery, trimmed and sliced
4 cloves garlic, peeled and crushed
3 strips thinly pared orange rind
½ level teaspoon fennel seeds
½ level teaspoon dried thyme
1 bay leaf
2 medium onions, peeled and quartered
8 medium carrots, peeled and sliced
6oz (175g) shelled fresh (or frozen) peas
3 level tablespoons chopped fresh basil
2 tablespoons tomato purée

*The classic combination
of tomatoes and basil
adds a distinctive
undertone to this dish,
giving a Mediterranean
character to the
traditional, full-bodied
beef stew.*

1 Season the beef with pepper. Heat the oil
in a large, heavy-based saucepan and toss the
meat in it over a high heat for 4-5 minutes.
Spoon the beef onto a plate and set aside.

2 Pour the wine into the pan and boil for
2 minutes, stirring to mix in the browned
juices. Stir in the stock, tomatoes, celery, half
the garlic, the orange rind, fennel seeds, thyme
and bay leaf, and bring to the boil. Put back the
beef, cover and simmer for 1 hour 15 minutes.

3 Discard the bay leaf, stir in the onions and
carrots, cover and simmer for 35 minutes. Test
the beef with a fork and if not quite tender,
cook for 15 minutes more. When it is tender,
add the peas and cook for 10 minutes more.

4 Mix the basil, tomato purée and remaining
garlic into the stew and reheat for 1 minute.

Pasta or chunks of crusty bread are the best
companions for the savoury stew.

Roast beef with Yorkshire puddings and mushroom gravy

SERVES 6
PREPARATION TIME: 30 minutes
COOKING TIME: 1 hour 20 minutes
OVEN: Preheat to 230°C (450°F, gas mark 8)

1½ lb (680g) lean topside beef, wiped
½ level teaspoon each plain flour, mustard powder and ground allspice

For the Yorkshire puddings:
3oz (85g) plain flour
1 egg, size 2
¼ pint (150ml) skimmed milk
1 teaspoon vegetable oil

For the mushroom gravy:
½ pint (285ml) vegetable stock
8oz (225g) chestnut mushrooms, wiped and finely chopped
1 level tablespoon cornflour
1 teaspoon Worcestershire sauce
1 level teaspoon French or whole-grain mustard
Freshly ground black pepper

1 Put the beef in a small roasting tin. Mix the flour, mustard and allspice together and rub all over the beef. Cook in the heated oven for 20 minutes, then lower the temperature to 190°C (375°F, gas mark 5) and cook for a further 40 minutes for medium-rare beef or 50 minutes for well-done beef. Baste with the meat juices two or three times during cooking.

2 As soon as the meat goes in the oven, prepare the pudding batter. Whisk together the flour, egg and half the milk until smooth. Gradually whisk in the remaining milk. Cover and leave to stand.

3 To prepare the gravy, simmer the stock and mushrooms in a saucepan, uncovered, for 15 minutes. Take off the heat and set aside.

4 When the beef is cooked to taste, lift it onto a hot serving dish, cover and leave to rest.

5 Raise the oven temperature to 220°C (425°F, gas mark 7). Brush a 12-cup, nonstick bun tray very lightly with the vegetable oil and heat for 1 minute in the oven. Pour a little of the batter into each cup, dividing it as equally as possible, and cook for 10 minutes or until well risen and golden brown.

6 Meanwhile, blend a little of the mushroom stock with the cornflour and stir back into the pan with the Worcestershire sauce and mustard. Skim off the fat from the meat tin and discard. Pour the mushroom mixture into the meat tin and stir briskly over a direct heat to blend in the browned meat juices as the gravy comes to the boil. Cook for 1 minute, then season with pepper and pour into a warmed serving jug.

Trim the joint of any fat before carving it into thin slices and arranging it on a serving plate. A garnish of bay or basil leaves gives a touch of colour for an attractive presentation. Give each diner two of the Yorkshire puddings with the beef and hand round the gravy separately.

ONE SERVING
CALORIES 240
TOTAL FAT 8g
SATURATED FAT 3g
CARBOHYDRATES 15g
ADDED SUGAR 0
FIBRE 1g
SODIUM 115mg

> **TIP**
> When mixing the Yorkshire pudding batter, use a balloon whisk. It produces a smooth batter quickly, and also incorporates tiny air bubbles in the mixture, which lighten the puddings.

Topside, one of the most popular cuts of beef, is an excellent source of lean meat and suitable for roasting or pot roasting. It is well-flavoured and, if properly kept by the butcher, makes a tender joint. In this recipe, a piquant mushroom gravy adds a new element to a traditional Sunday lunch.

Sirloin steak with basil sauce

SERVES 4
PREPARATION TIME: 15 minutes
COOKING TIME: 25 minutes

1lb (450g) sirloin steak, cut in one thick
piece, fat removed
Freshly ground black pepper
4oz (115g) shallots or onion, peeled and chopped
3 tablespoons water
12oz (340g) courgettes, trimmed and
coarsely grated
1 tablespoon olive oil
2 level teaspoons capers, drained and chopped
3 level tablespoons chopped fresh basil

1 Wipe the steak with kitchen paper, sprinkle it with pepper and set it aside.

2 Boil the shallots or onion in a medium saucepan with the water until they are transparent and the water is reduced by half. Stir in the courgettes and oil, cover and cook over a low heat for 8-10 minutes, stirring frequently, until the courgettes are soft.

3 Pass the vegetables through a food mill or blend in a food processor. Stir in the capers and basil, and season with pepper. Reheat the sauce, spoon into a serving dish, cover and keep hot.

4 Heat a heavy frying pan and sear the steak in it over a high heat for 30 seconds on each side. Turn down the heat and cook the meat for about 8 minutes for medium-rare, turning it once or twice. Cook for 1-2 minutes more on each side if you prefer steak well done.

5 Cut the steak downwards and slanting into thin slices and serve with the basil sauce.

This simply made but luxurious dish needs only a mixed leafy salad and french bread with it. You can garnish the meat and sauce with parsley sprigs and whole capers if you wish.

ONE SERVING

CALORIES 200

TOTAL FAT 9g

SATURATED FAT 3g

CARBOHYDRATES 4g

ADDED SUGAR 0

FIBRE 1g

SODIUM 90mg

The peppery clove flavour of basil and the pungency of capers are combined in the thick sauce that spices this plainly cooked steak.

Fillet steak with wild mushrooms

SERVES 4
PREPARATION TIME: 20 minutes
COOKING TIME: 15 minutes

1 teaspoon olive oil
1lb (450g) fillet steak, cut into 4 slices
Freshly ground black pepper

2 tablespoons whisky
7oz (200g) fresh wild mushrooms, cleaned and
sliced, or dried porcini, soaked and sliced
1 bay leaf
1 clove garlic, peeled and crushed
1 level teaspoon plain flour
4oz (115g) low-fat natural yoghurt

Whisky and the rich juice of wild mushrooms give a warm, nutty flavour to the smooth and tart yoghurt sauce.

1 Heat the oil in a nonstick frying pan. Season the steaks with pepper and sear them on both sides over a high heat, then lower the heat to moderate and cook 2-3 minutes each side for rare meat, 3-4 for medium, 4-5 for well done.

2 Pour the whisky over the steaks and boil it for 1-2 minutes until reduced by half. Lift the steaks onto a heated plate, cover and keep hot.

3 Put the mushrooms in the pan with the bay leaf and garlic. Cover and cook quickly for 2-3 minutes, then uncover and boil until the juices have reduced by half. Blend the flour with the yoghurt until smooth. Stir the mixture into the mushrooms and heat without boiling until the sauce thickens. Season it with pepper and discard the bay leaf. Pour the mushroom sauce over the steaks and serve immediately.

Hot red cabbage and a wild rice mixture are perfect foils for the tender meat and rich sauce. You can add a sprig of bay, basil or sage for a touch of colour.

> **TIP**
> *Remove the stalks from the mushrooms and use in a soup or stew. They are tougher than the stalks of cultivated mushrooms and could spoil the succulent dish.*

Oriental steak

ONE SERVING

CALORIES 200

TOTAL FAT 8g

SATURATED FAT 2g

CARBOHYDRATES 6g

ADDED SUGAR 5g

FIBRE 0g

SODIUM 70mg

SERVES 4
PREPARATION TIME: 5 minutes, plus 12 hours to marinate
COOKING TIME: 10 minutes

1lb (450g) rump steak in one slice, fat removed
2 tablespoons soy sauce
1 level tablespoon soft brown sugar
1 tablespoon lemon juice

2 level teaspoons Dijon mustard
2 level teaspoons peeled and grated root ginger
2 cloves garlic, peeled and crushed
2 teaspoons sesame oil
3 tablespoons dry sherry or white wine
Freshly ground black pepper
2 tablespoons white vinegar
1 level teaspoon granulated sugar
2 tablespoons water

The steak absorbs the gingered sherry marinade which tenderises the meat and imparts a distinctly Eastern flavour, subtly enhanced by soy sauce and sesame oil.

1 Put the steak in a shallow glass or china dish that will just hold it and prick all over with a fork. Mix the soy sauce, brown sugar, lemon juice, mustard, ginger, garlic, sesame oil and half the sherry or wine, season with pepper and pour over the steak. Cover and refrigerate for about 12 hours, turning the meat a few times.

2 Take the steak out of the marinade and pat it dry with kitchen paper. Use a sharp knife to score it with crisscross cuts. Heat a frying pan and cook the steak over a moderately high heat, without fat or oil, for 3 minutes each side for rare, 4 for medium or 5 for well done. Lift the steak onto a heated serving dish.

3 Let the frying pan cool slightly before adding the remaining sherry or wine, the vinegar, granulated sugar and water. Boil, stirring all the time, until the mixture has reduced to about 2 tablespoons of concentrated glaze.

4 Cut downwards and slanting through the meat to carve it into thin slices. Spoon a little of the glaze onto each serving.

Serve the steak with a dish of lightly cooked Chinese noodles, tossed with a little sesame oil to continue the Oriental style of the dish. A raw vegetable salad and a parsley garnish add crispness and colour.

Peppered sirloin steak

SERVES 6
PREPARATION TIME: 10 minutes
COOKING TIME: 10 minutes
OVEN: Preheat to 240°C (475°F, gas mark 9)

1½ lb (680g) sirloin steak, cut in one thick slice, fat removed
2 level tablespoons black peppercorns, crushed
1 tablespoon olive oil
3 spring onions, trimmed and finely chopped
2 tablespoons dry white wine
8fl oz (225ml) beef stock

1 Coat both sides of the steak with the crushed peppercorns.

2 Heat the oil in a heavy-based flameproof casserole over a very high heat and quickly sear the steak in it, for about 30 seconds on each side.

3 Put the casserole in the heated oven and roast the steak, uncovered, for 4-5 minutes for rare, 6-7 for medium, and 7-8 for well done. Lift the steak onto a heated serving dish and carve downwards and slanting into thin slices.

4 Stir the spring onions into the meat juices and cook over a direct heat for 30 seconds. Add the wine and cook, uncovered, for 1 minute before adding the beef stock and simmering for 2-3 minutes while scraping the hardened juices into the sauce. Boil to reduce to about half a cupful and pour round the steak.

Lightly steamed sugar snap peas and carrots provide a crisp, sweet contrast to the tender, peppery steak. Serve warm wholemeal rolls (see p.366) with the dish for mopping up the juices. If you like, you can garnish the dish with a few bay or sage leaves.

TIP
To crush the peppercorns without a mortar and pestle, put them inside a double-thickness polythene bag and roll firmly on a sturdy board with a rolling pin.

A crust of crunchy peppercorns seals in the juices of the lean sirloin, keeping beautifully moist a cut which can sometimes be dry. The meat's full flavour comes through the hot pungency of the crust.

Beef parcels with chestnuts and red wine

SERVES 4
PREPARATION TIME: 30 minutes
COOKING TIME: 1 hour
OVEN: Preheat to 160°C (325°F, gas mark 3)

4oz (115g) chestnuts, shell and inner skin removed, finely chopped
2oz (60g) mushrooms, wiped and finely chopped
1 small carrot, peeled and grated
1 clove garlic, peeled and crushed
1 level tablespoon whole-grain mustard
2 level teaspoons chopped fresh thyme
⅛ level teaspoon salt
Freshly ground black pepper
4 slices braising beef, each about 4oz (115g), fat removed, beaten out thin
Thin string to tie parcels
1 tablespoon olive oil
3 shallots or small onions, peeled and finely sliced
1 level tablespoon plain flour
¼ pint (150ml) red wine
¼ pint (150ml) vegetable or beef stock

1   Mix together thoroughly the chestnuts, mushrooms, carrot, garlic, mustard, thyme and salt, and season with pepper. Spread out the beef slices on a board and spoon a quarter of the chestnut mixture onto the centre of each. Wrap the meat round the stuffing to make four neat parcels and tie with clean, thin string.

2   Heat the oil in a flameproof casserole and brown the parcels in it over a high heat. Lift them out with a slotted spoon and set aside. Cook the shallots or onions in the casserole gently for 2-3 minutes. Stir in the flour and cook for 1 minute, then gradually stir in the wine and stock and continue stirring while the sauce comes to the boil and thickens.

3   Return the beef parcels to the casserole, cover and cook in the heated oven for 1 hour. Carefully snip and remove the string when you serve the parcels.

Cauliflower, baked tomatoes and jacket potatoes go well with the moist beef parcels. You can use ale in place of the wine and, when chestnuts are out of season, soaked and chopped dried chestnuts can replace them. If you gather your own chestnuts, be sure they are sweet chestnuts, not horse chestnuts.

ONE SERVING	
CALORIES 275	
TOTAL FAT 10g	
SATURATED FAT 3g	
CARBOHYDRATES 16g	
ADDED SUGAR 0	
FIBRE 2g	
SODIUM 140mg	

TIP
Chestnuts peel easily if you cut a deep cross in the top of each, put them in a pan with cold water to cover, bring to the boil and simmer for 10 minutes. Spoon out one at a time to peel.

The sweet chestnut stuffing and the rich wine sauce are delicious accompaniments to the thinly beaten slices of beef. They combine to make an unusual autumn dish.

Beef kebabs with courgettes and tomatoes

SERVES 4
PREPARATION TIME: 20 minutes, plus 3 hours
to marinate
COOKING TIME: 15 minutes

4 level tablespoons low-fat natural yoghurt
2 tablespoons lemon juice
2 cloves garlic, peeled and finely chopped
2 level teaspoons peeled and grated root ginger,
or ½ level teaspoon ground ginger
2 level teaspoons paprika
½ level teaspoon each cayenne pepper, ground
nutmeg, cumin and coriander
1lb (450g) rump steak with fat removed,
cut into 12 cubes
1 medium courgette, trimmed and cut into 12 slices
1 large red pepper, de-seeded and cut
into 12 squares
4 long metal skewers
8 cherry tomatoes
2 small onions, peeled and cut into quarters
Fresh coriander leaves to garnish

1 Mix the yoghurt, lemon juice, garlic and
ginger with the paprika, cayenne pepper,
nutmeg, cumin and coriander. Whisk the
mixture well, or blend it in a food processor
for 10 seconds.

2 Pour the mixture into a glass or china bowl
and turn the beef cubes in it to coat well. Cover
and put in the refrigerator for 3 hours to
marinate. Turn the meat once during this time.

3 Blanch the courgette and pepper for one
minute in boiling water.

4 Lift the beef cubes out of the marinade and
thread onto four oiled skewers, with a share of
the courgette, red pepper, tomatoes and onion.
Lay the kebabs on the grill rack and cook under
a high heat for 15-20 minutes, frequently
brushing with the marinade and turning until
the meat and vegetables are tender. Reduce the
heat if the kebabs are browning too much.

Serve the kebabs very hot, still on their skewers,
on a bed of boiled green lentils and garnished
with fresh coriander. A dish of diced cucumber
mixed with low-fat natural yoghurt is a
welcome cool accompaniment to the spicy
kebabs. For a summer meal, you might prefer
rolls and a leafy salad with the kebabs.

ONE SERVING	
CALORIES 185	
TOTAL FAT 6g	
SATURATED FAT 3g	
CARBOHYDRATES 8g	
ADDED SUGAR 0	
FIBRE 1g	
SODIUM 90mg	

*Marinating meat in yoghurt and lemon juice makes
it a fittingly tender partner for the vegetables in this
colourful dish. Here the yoghurt is warmly spiced.*

Lamb and asparagus stir-fry

SERVES 4
PREPARATION TIME: 20 minutes, plus 30 minutes
to marinate
COOKING TIME: 15 minutes

ONE SERVING
CALORIES 330
TOTAL FAT 18g
SATURATED FAT 5g
CARBOHYDRATES 12g
ADDED SUGAR 0
FIBRE 3g
SODIUM 660mg

2 level tablespoons peeled and grated root ginger,
or 1 level teaspoon ground ginger
2 cloves garlic, peeled and crushed
2 tablespoons soy sauce
2 tablespoons dry sherry
2 tablespoons sesame oil
1lb (450g) lamb without bone or fat, cut into strips
1lb (450g) thin asparagus, trimmed and cut
diagonally into short lengths

1 Spanish onion, peeled, quartered and sliced
1 medium green pepper, de-seeded and sliced
1 level teaspoon cornflour
3fl oz (85ml) chicken or vegetable stock (see p.19)
3oz (85g) bamboo shoots
3oz (85g) water chestnuts, thinly sliced

1 Combine the ginger, garlic, soy sauce, sherry
and 1 teaspoon of the sesame oil in a glass or
china dish. Stir the lamb into this marinade,
cover and leave in a cool place for 30 minutes.

2 Heat 1 tablespoon of the sesame oil in
a large frying pan over a high heat and stir-fry
the asparagus in it for 3-5 minutes until just
becoming tender. Add the onion and green
pepper and stir-fry for 1 minute more, then
cover and cook for 1 minute. Using a slotted
spoon, lift all the vegetables onto a large plate.

3 Heat the remaining sesame oil in the pan
over a high heat and stir in the lamb. Pour on
the marinade and cook, stirring, for 5 minutes.
Blend the cornflour with the stock, stir into the
pan juices and boil until the liquid thickens.

4 Put the vegetables back in the pan, mix in
the bamboo shoots and water chestnuts
and toss over a moderate heat for 2 minutes.

Serve the stir-fry while piping hot with plenty
of fluffed-up rice.

*Young asparagus stalks are ideal for stir-frying and
their delicate flavour suits that of the lamb. Bamboo
shoots and water chestnuts add satisfying crunchiness.*

Lamb baked in aubergines

ONE SERVING
CALORIES 195
TOTAL FAT 9g
SATURATED FAT 4g
CARBOHYDRATES 8g
ADDED SUGAR 0
FIBRE 3g
SODIUM 185mg

SERVES 4
PREPARATION TIME: 20 minutes, plus 30 minutes
to stand
COOKING TIME: 1 hour 5 minutes
OVEN: Preheat to 190°C (375°F, gas mark 5)

2 medium aubergines
¼ level teaspoon salt
1 teaspoon olive oil
1 onion, peeled and chopped

2 cloves garlic, peeled and chopped
12oz (340g) lamb without bone or fat, minced
1 level teaspoon each ground cumin and coriander
2 level teaspoons plain flour
7oz (200g) tinned chopped tomatoes
1oz (30g) pine nuts, lightly toasted
2 level tablespoons chopped fresh parsley
Freshly ground black pepper
2 level tablespoons fresh brown breadcrumbs
Lime wedges and coriander sprigs to garnish

Aubergines acting as edible gratin dishes provide a tinge of bitterness to offset the sweetness of the filling.

1 Halve the aubergines lengthways, score the cut surfaces crisscross fashion, sprinkle with the salt and leave to stand for 30 minutes.

2 Rinse the aubergines with plenty of cold water, pat them dry and put them cut side down on a sheet of nonstick baking paper on a baking sheet. Prick the skin all over and bake in the heated oven for 30 minutes.

3 Meanwhile, heat the oil in a heavy-based saucepan and toss the onion and garlic in it over a high heat until golden. Stir in the lamb and cook briskly until it begins to brown. Break up any lumps that form with a fork.

4 Sprinkle on the cumin, coriander and flour and cook, stirring, for 30 seconds. Pour in the tomatoes and bring to the boil, then stir, cover and simmer for about 10 minutes.

5 When the aubergines are tender, scoop out the flesh leaving shells about ¼ in (6mm) thick. Chop the flesh and stir it into the lamb along with the pine nuts and chopped parsley. Season the mixture with pepper.

6 Fill the aubergine shells with the lamb mixture, arrange them in an ovenproof dish and sprinkle on the breadcrumbs. Pour a thin covering of water into the bottom of the dish. Bake the filled aubergines in the heated oven for about 50 minutes, or until they are crisp and golden brown on top.

Garnish the aubergines with the lime wedges and coriander and serve with bulgur wheat simmered with a few sultanas to emphasise the Balkan flavour of the dish. Side salads of tomato and onion sprinkled with snipped dill fronds or parsley will provide a sharp contrast.

Lamb and barley stew

SERVES 4
PREPARATION TIME: 15 minutes
COOKING TIME: 1 hour 45 minutes

2 teaspoons olive oil
1lb (450g) meat from boned leg of lamb
or neck fillet with fat removed, cut into cubes
1 onion, peeled and sliced
1 clove garlic, peeled and chopped
1½ pints (850ml) chicken or vegetable
stock
2oz (60g) pearl barley
Freshly ground black pepper
1 turnip, peeled and cut into wedges
2 large carrots, peeled and sliced
2 medium leeks, sliced and washed
2 sticks celery, trimmed and sliced
2 level tablespoons chopped fresh parsley

1 Heat the oil in a heavy-based saucepan and toss the lamb, onion and garlic in it over a moderate heat for 5 minutes, until browning.

2 Pour in the stock, stir in the barley, season with pepper and bring to the boil. Reduce the heat, cover the saucepan and simmer for 1 hour, stirring from time to time.

3 Mix in the turnip, carrots, leeks and celery, cover and cook for 40 minutes, or until the vegetables are tender. Scatter on the parsley just before serving in warmed individual bowls.

Steamed potatoes and savoy cabbage go well with the stew. You can steam the potatoes on top of the stew, sitting the steamer on top of the pan for the last 30 minutes of cooking.

ONE SERVING	
CALORIES 295	
TOTAL FAT 13g	
SATURATED FAT 5g	
CARBOHYDRATES 20g	
ADDED SUGAR 0	
FIBRE 3g	
SODIUM 120mg	

TIP
Buy 1½ lb (680g)
of meat to give the
right amount after
boning and
trimming.

There is a north-country character about this hearty stew, which is flavoured with winter vegetables and thickened with pearl barley.

Lamb stew with carrots and runner beans

SERVES 4
PREPARATION TIME: 30 minutes
COOKING TIME: 1 hour 10 minutes

2 tablespoons olive oil
1lb (450g) meat from chump ends or lean shoulder
of lamb with bone and fat removed, cut into cubes
12-16 small shallots or pickling onions, peeled
1 clove garlic, peeled and crushed

2 level tablespoons plain flour
¾ pint (425ml) vegetable or beef stock
1 level tablespoon chopped fresh marjoram,
or 1 level teaspoon dried marjoram
Freshly ground black pepper
2 medium carrots, peeled and diced
4 medium potatoes, peeled and cut into chunks
6oz (175g) runner beans, trimmed and
sliced diagonally

ONE SERVING	
CALORIES	385
TOTAL FAT	18g
SATURATED FAT	6g
CARBOHYDRATES	30g
ADDED SUGAR	0
FIBRE	4g
SODIUM	115mg

1 Heat the oil in a large, heavy-based saucepan and toss the lamb cubes in it over a high heat for about 5 minutes, until browned all over. Lift out the lamb with a slotted spoon and put it to drain on kitchen paper.

2 Cook the shallots or onions in the saucepan over a high heat, stirring, for about 4 minutes until browned, then mix in the garlic and cook for about 30 seconds.

3 Pour off the fat from the saucepan and discard. Stir the flour into the browned vegetables and cook over a moderate heat for 1 minute before gradually blending in the

stock. Stir to loosen the browned cooking juices from the base of the pan while the sauce comes to the boil and thickens.

4 Put the lamb back in the pan, sprinkle on the marjoram and season with pepper. Bring to the boil, stirring, then turn down the heat, cover the saucepan and simmer for 30 minutes.

5 Mix in the carrots and potatoes and cook for 15 minutes, then stir in the green beans and simmer for a further 10 minutes.

Serve the stew in individual heated bowls with warm, crusty french bread.

Browning the meat before stewing improves both the colour and taste of this stew. It is worth spending time trimming chump ends or shoulder because of their sweet meat.

Herbed lamb cutlets

SERVES 4
PREPARATION TIME: 5 minutes
COOKING TIME: 8 minutes

8 lamb cutlets, each about 4oz (115g), fat trimmed
2 cloves garlic, peeled and halved
1 tablespoon olive oil
1 level tablespoon chopped mixed fresh thyme,
marjoram and rosemary, or 1 level teaspoon dried
mixed herbs
Freshly ground black pepper
Fresh mint and lemon wedges to garnish

1 Lay the cutlets in a shallow dish and rub all over with the cut side of the garlic cloves. Brush both sides of the cutlets with the oil, coat with the herbs and season with pepper.

2 Place the cutlets on the grill rack and cook under a high heat for 4 minutes on each side. Arrange them on warmed serving plates and garnish with the mint and lemon.

Serve with new potatoes and a green salad, and let the diners remove any remaining fat.

TIP
To enhance the herb flavour of the cutlets, coat them 4-5 hours before cooking, cover the dish and put in the refrigerator to marinate.

For ease of preparation and freshness of taste, nothing beats young and tender lamb cutlets briefly grilled in a coating of lively herbs.

Lancashire hotpot

ONE SERVING

CALORIES 360

TOTAL FAT 12g

SATURATED FAT 5g

CARBOHYDRATES 39g

ADDED SUGAR 0

FIBRE 4g

SODIUM 120mg

Long, slow cooking lets the vegetables absorb the flavour of the meltingly tender lamb, and creates a warmly satisfying winter dish.

SERVES 4
PREPARATION TIME: 20 minutes
COOKING TIME: 2 hours 15 minutes
OVEN: Preheat to 180°C (350°F, gas mark 4)

8 middle or best end of neck lamb chops,
about 2lb (900g) together, fat removed
2 bay leaves
1 level tablespoon chopped fresh mixed herbs,
or 1 level teaspoon dried mixed herbs
Freshly ground black pepper
1 pint (570ml) beef or vegetable stock
1 large onion, peeled and sliced
2 medium carrots, peeled and sliced
1 large leek, trimmed, sliced and washed
1½ lb (680g) potatoes, peeled and thickly sliced
1 teaspoon olive oil

1 Arrange the lamb chops in a casserole. Tuck 1 bay leaf underneath and 1 on top, sprinkle on the herbs and season with pepper. Pour in just enough of the stock to cover the meat.

2 Spread the onion, carrots and leek over the chops and season with pepper. Lay overlapping slices of potato on top of the vegetables and brush sparingly with the olive oil.

3 Cover the casserole and cook in the heated oven for 1 hour 30 minutes, then uncover and cook for 45 minutes more to brown the top. Remove the bay leaves as you serve the hotpot.

Lightly cooked cabbage or sautéed brussels sprouts make a crisp contrast to the hotpot.

Kidneys Creole

ONE SERVING

CALORIES 205

TOTAL FAT 8g

SATURATED FAT 2g

CARBOHYDRATES 9g

ADDED SUGAR 3g

FIBRE 2g

SODIUM 320mg

TIP
To remove the white core easily from a kidney, snip it out with kitchen scissors.

SERVES 4
PREPARATION TIME: 10 minutes
COOKING TIME: 20 minutes

1 tablespoon olive oil
2 level teaspoons peeled and grated root ginger, or ¼ level teaspoon ground ginger
1 clove garlic, peeled and crushed
1 small onion, peeled and finely chopped
2oz (60g) button mushrooms, wiped and sliced
1¼ lb (550g) lambs' kidneys, skinned, halved and cored
1lb (450g) tomatoes, skinned and chopped
½ medium green pepper, de-seeded and diced
½ medium red pepper, de-seeded and diced
2 teaspoons tomato purée
2 level teaspoons muscavado or soft brown sugar
1 tablespoon raspberry vinegar
1 tablespoon lime juice
½ teaspoon hot pepper sauce
Freshly ground black pepper

1 Heat the oil in a frying pan and cook the ginger, garlic and onion in it over a moderate heat for 2-3 minutes. Stir in the mushrooms and cook for 1 minute. Add the kidneys and brown over a high heat, stirring, for 5 minutes.

2 Stir in the tomatoes, green and red peppers, tomato purée, sugar, raspberry vinegar, lime juice and hot pepper sauce. When the mixture comes to the boil, season with pepper, lower the heat and simmer, uncovered, for 10 minutes or until the kidneys are just cooked through.

Serve the kidneys with fluffy rice; you can give a touch of colour with fresh parsley sprigs.

Delicate kidneys are enlivened by a hot sauce with the tomatoes, onions and peppers of Creole cooking sharpened by raspberry vinegar and lime juice.

Lamb's liver with orange and onion

SERVES 4
PREPARATION TIME: 15 minutes
COOKING TIME: 30 minutes
OVEN: Preheat to 180°C (350°F, gas mark 4)

1 tablespoon olive oil
1¼ lb (550g) lamb's liver, very thinly sliced
1 large onion, peeled, sliced and separated into rings

1 level tablespoon plain flour
½ pint (285ml) chicken stock
Grated rind and juice of half a small orange
1 level tablespoon chopped fresh thyme or marjoram, or 1 level teaspoon dried thyme or marjoram
Freshly ground black pepper
Orange rind and thyme sprigs to garnish

Braised lamb's liver produces a rich gravy, which is given an edge here with orange and sweetened with thyme.

TIP
To prevent liver from curling during cooking, remove its fine outer membrane. Ease away a corner with the tip of a knife then gently pull the membrane off.

---

1 Heat the oil in a frying pan and brown the liver in it quickly on each side over a fairly high heat. Remove the liver from the pan and set aside on kitchen paper to drain. Cook the onion gently in the frying pan, stirring occasionally, until lightly browned.

2 Stir in the flour and cook for 1 minute before gradually stirring in the stock. Bring to the boil, stirring continuously, then add the orange rind, orange juice and herbs, season with pepper, and simmer for 1 minute.

3 Pour two-thirds of the onion sauce into a shallow ovenproof serving dish. Arrange the slices of liver on top in one layer and spoon the rest of the sauce over them.

4 Cover the dish with a lid or foil and bake in the heated oven for 30 minutes, until the liver is just cooked through. Garnish with the orange rind and thyme sprigs.

Serve rice with the liver and give colour and bite with lightly cooked carrots and broccoli.

Stuffed leg of lamb with orange sauce

SERVES 8
PREPARATION TIME: 25 minutes
COOKING TIME: 2 hours 30 minutes–3 hours
OVEN: Preheat to 230°C (450°F, gas mark 8)

1 tablespoon olive oil
1 large onion, peeled and finely chopped
4 cloves garlic, peeled and crushed
1lb (450g) button mushrooms, wiped and chopped
2oz (60g) wholemeal bread with crusts cut off, diced
1oz (30g) fresh parsley, finely chopped
1 level teaspoon dried marjoram
½ level teaspoon dried basil
1 medium orange
Freshly ground black pepper
6lb (2.7kg) leg of lamb, bone and fat removed
1 level tablespoon plain flour
½ pint (285ml) vegetable or beef stock
Orange wedges and sprigs of marjoram to garnish

1 Heat the oil in a large frying pan and cook the onion and garlic in it gently for 5 minutes, until lightly coloured. Add the mushrooms and cook for a further 8 minutes, or until the mushroom juices have evaporated.

2 Take the pan off the heat and mix in the bread, parsley, marjoram and basil. Grate in about 1 teaspoon of rind from the orange, season with pepper and stir well.

3 Stuff the lamb with the mushroom mixture, packing the stuffing, not too tightly, along the cavity left by removing the bone. Secure with skewers or thin, clean string if necessary to hold the meat in shape.

4 Put the lamb on a rack in a shallow roasting tin and roast in the heated oven, uncovered, for 15 minutes. Reduce the oven temperature to 180°C (350°F, gas mark 4), and continue cooking for another 2 hours for meat that is slightly pink and 2 hours 20 minutes for well-done meat.

5 Pare off the skin and outer membrane of the orange with a very sharp knife. Free the segments by cutting down each side of them to remove the membranes.

6 When the lamb is cooked, lift it onto a warmed serving dish, cover with foil and leave to rest for 10 minutes. Skim off and discard the fat from the juices in the roasting tin. Mix the flour into the remaining juices and gradually stir in the stock. Bring to the boil over a low heat, stirring to incorporate the browned juices from the bottom of the tin. Reduce the heat and simmer for 5 minutes, stirring frequently. Add the orange segments and heat through for 1 minute, then pour into a heated sauceboat.

7 Uncover the lamb and remove any skewers and string. Slice the meat, not too thinly, leaving the diners to remove any remaining fat. Garnish with the orange wedges and marjoram. Serve with the sauce.

The traditional accompaniments of new potatoes and peas cannot be bettered, but you can offer a different look with mangetout or sugar snap peas.

ONE SERVING

CALORIES 335

TOTAL FAT 18g

SATURATED FAT 7g

CARBOHYDRATES 7g

ADDED SUGAR 0

FIBRE 2g

SODIUM 285mg

TIP
Push the stuffing into the leg cavity with a wooden spoon, using the handle end if necessary to reach the centre.

A mushroom stuffing, seasoned with onion, garlic and herbs, and a sauce infused with orange juice and zest, moisten the meat and sharpen the mild flavour of the roast lamb. The leg, a popular cut, provides plenty of tender, lean meat, delicious hot or cold.

Indonesian-style pork kebabs

SERVES 4
PREPARATION TIME: 20 minutes, plus 1 hour to marinate
COOKING TIME: 20 minutes

ONE SERVING
CALORIES 205
TOTAL FAT 11g
SATURATED FAT 2g
CARBOHYDRATES 5g
ADDED SUGAR 3g
FIBRE 1g
SODIUM 160mg

½ level teaspoon ground ginger
2 cloves garlic, peeled
1 small onion, peeled and chopped
1 teaspoon soy sauce
2 level tablespoons unsalted peanuts, toasted
1 teaspoon olive oil
2 level teaspoons soft brown sugar

2 teaspoons lemon juice
½ level teaspoon each ground coriander, cumin and cinnamon
2 tablespoons water
12oz (340g) pork tenderloin, trimmed of fat and cut into cubes
4 metal or wooden skewers
Finely shredded lemon rind, spring onion and parsley leaves to garnish

1 Put the ginger, garlic, onion, soy sauce, peanuts, oil, sugar, lemon juice, coriander, cumin and cinnamon in a food processor with the water. Blend for 8-10 seconds, until smooth, then pour into a glass or china dish. Stir the pork cubes into the mixture, cover and put in the refrigerator to marinate for 1 hour.

2 Thread the meat onto the skewers, ensuring that the cubes do not touch one another.

3 Lay the kebabs on a grill rack and brush them with the marinade. Grill for about 20 minutes under a high heat, turning and brushing with the marinade several times, until the pork is cooked through. Arrange the kebabs on a heated serving dish and garnish with the lemon rind, spring onion and parsley.

Boiled rice provides a simple base for the richly flavoured meat, and a crunchy bean sprout and pepper salad refreshes the palate.

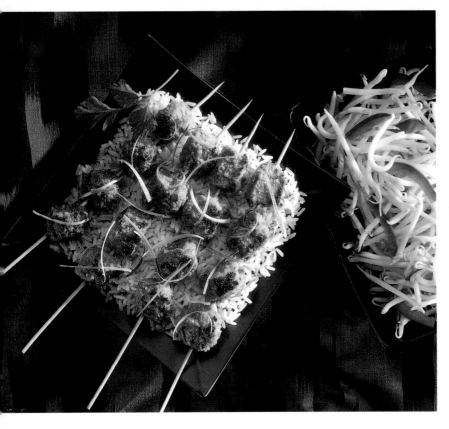

The spicy peanut marinade gives an exotic taste of the East to beautifully tender morsels of pork grilled on skewers to brown every side to perfection.

Stuffed loin of pork

ONE SERVING
CALORIES 345
TOTAL FAT 14g
SATURATED FAT 4g
CARBOHYDRATES 12g
ADDED SUGAR 0
FIBRE 2g
SODIUM 185mg

SERVES 4
PREPARATION TIME: 25 minutes
COOKING TIME: 45 minutes
OVEN: Preheat to 200°C (400°F, gas mark 6)

2 tablespoons olive oil
2 tablespoons water
1 large onion, peeled and chopped
1 large carrot, peeled and finely chopped

1 medium red pepper, de-seeded and finely chopped
Freshly ground black pepper
1oz (30g) wholemeal breadcrumbs
1 level teaspoon ground ginger
⅛ level teaspoon ground cloves
1½ lb (680g) rolled loin of pork, trimmed of fat
2 tablespoons lemon juice
7fl oz (200ml) vegetable or chicken stock

The pork is trimmed of fat but, moistened from within by a savoury stuffing and from outside by stock, it cooks to tempting succulence.

1 Heat one tablespoon of the oil in a frying pan with the water and cook the onion, carrot and red pepper in it over a low heat for 6-8 minutes, until the vegetables are soft. Season with black pepper and stir in the breadcrumbs, ginger and cloves to make a well-blended stuffing.

2 Cut a pocket in the centre of the pork for the filling. Push in the stuffing, but not too tightly or it will be squeezed out as the meat shrinks during cooking. Sprinkle the lemon juice over the meat and rub it in well.

3 Heat the remaining oil in a small roasting tin over a moderately high direct heat and quickly brown the stuffed pork all over. Pour the stock in with the meat and bring it to the boil, then put the tin in the heated oven and cook the pork for 20 minutes. Lower the heat to 180°C (350°F, gas mark 4) and cook for another 20 minutes, basting from time to time with the stock, until the pork is cooked through.

4 Lift the pork onto a hot serving plate, cover it loosely with foil and leave it to rest for 10 minutes. Skim off and discard the fat from the juices in the roasting tin.

5 Reheat the roasting juices while you cut the meat into slices. Spoon the juices round the meat before serving.

New potatoes, mangetout and tiny sweetcorn cobs add bite and extra colour to the tender slices of pork.

> **TIP**
> *To make the pocket for the stuffing, push a very sharp long-bladed knife through the centre of the meat from end to end. Move the knife gently from side to side until the slit is large enough to hold the stuffing.*

Apple and cider, popular ingredients in the cooking of Normandy, mellow the lively herb flavouring in the sauce as well as the meatballs.

Normandy meatballs and cider sauce

SERVES 4
PREPARATION TIME: 15 minutes
COOKING TIME: 25 minutes
OVEN: Preheat to 200°C (400°F, gas mark 6)

1lb (450g) boneless pork with fat removed, minced
3oz (85g) wholemeal breadcrumbs
2oz (60g) ready-to-use stoned prunes, finely chopped
1 dessert apple, about 4oz (115g), peeled, cored and finely chopped
1oz (30g) walnuts, chopped
1 level tablespoon coarsely chopped fresh sage, or 1 level teaspoon dried sage
1/8 level teaspoon salt
Freshly ground black pepper
1 egg, size 2, lightly beaten
1/2 oz (15g) slightly salted butter
1 small onion, peeled and finely chopped
1 level tablespoon plain flour
1/4 pint (150ml) vegetable or chicken stock
1/4 pint (150ml) medium sweet cider
1 level tablespoon chopped fresh parsley
2 level tablespoons low-fat natural yoghurt
Sage leaves to garnish

1 Mix the pork, breadcrumbs, prunes, apple, walnuts and sage, season with salt and pepper and work in the egg to bind the mixture. Divide it into 20 pieces and roll each into a ball.

2 Put the pork balls into a nonstick roasting tin and cook in the heated oven for about 25 minutes, or until golden brown.

3 Meanwhile, melt the butter in a saucepan, and cook the onion in it gently for about 5 minutes, or until soft. Stir in the flour and cook for 30 seconds. Gradually stir in the stock and cider and bring to the boil, stirring continuously. Mix in the parsley, season with pepper and set the sauce aside.

4 When the meatballs are cooked, stir the yoghurt into the sauce and reheat, but do not boil or it will curdle. Pour into a warmed jug for serving. Turn the meatballs into a serving dish and garnish with sage leaves.

Mashed potato goes well with the meatballs, while crisp spring greens or broccoli will make a pleasing contrast with their tenderness.

Pork with roasted peppers

SERVES 4
PREPARATION TIME: 30 minutes
COOKING TIME: 25 minutes

2 large red peppers
1lb (450g) boned shoulder of pork with fat removed, cut into 4 slices
1 level tablespoon plain flour
1 tablespoon olive oil
1 medium onion, peeled and chopped
2 cloves garlic, peeled and crushed
2lb (900g) tinned tomatoes, drained and chopped
2oz (60g) sultanas
1 tablespoon red wine vinegar
¼ level teaspoon cayenne pepper
1 level teaspoon dried oregano

1 Grill the peppers under a moderate heat for 10-12 minutes, turning often, until they are browned all over. Put them in a bowl, cover with a clean damp cloth and set aside. When they are cool enough to handle, pull off their skins, working over a bowl to catch any juice. Remove the seeds and cut the flesh into strips.

2 Meanwhile, put the pork slices between sheets of greaseproof paper and beat them with a rolling pin until they are very thin. Coat the slices lightly with the flour.

3 Heat the oil in a frying pan, and cook the pork slices in it over a moderate heat for 4 minutes on each side. Lay the slices on a plate covered with kitchen paper and set aside.

4 Fry the onion and garlic gently in the same pan for 5 minutes, until softened. Stir in the tomatoes, sultanas, vinegar, cayenne pepper, oregano and any juice from the grilled peppers. Bring to the boil, reduce the heat, cover and cook for 5 minutes, stirring occasionally.

5 Put the pork slices in the sauce, scatter in the pepper strips, cover and heat through for about 5 minutes.

Fresh pasta and a mixed green salad make simple accompaniments for the subtly flavoured pork and its sauce.

ONE SERVING	
CALORIES	300
TOTAL FAT	9g
SATURATED FAT	2g
CARBOHYDRATES	27g
ADDED SUGAR	0
FIBRE	4g
SODIUM	185mg

Roasting the sweet red peppers enhances their characteristically smoky flavour. Partnered by tomatoes and sharpened by a little vinegar and cayenne, they give a vivid touch of the hot south to the pork.

Pork and red-cabbage casserole

SERVES 4
PREPARATION TIME: 35 minutes
COOKING TIME: 1 hour
OVEN: Preheat to 180°C (350°F, gas mark 4)

ONE SERVING	
CALORIES	230
TOTAL FAT	11g
SATURATED FAT	2g
CARBOHYDRATES	13g
ADDED SUGAR	0
FIBRE	3g
SODIUM	75mg

12oz (340g) boned pork shoulder with
fat removed, cut into cubes
2 level tablespoons plain flour
2 tablespoons olive oil
1 medium onion, peeled and thinly sliced
1 medium carrot, peeled and sliced
3 cloves garlic, peeled and crushed
1 large dessert apple, peeled, cored and sliced
6oz (175g) red cabbage, coarsely shredded
3 tablespoons red wine vinegar

4fl oz (115ml) chicken stock
7 allspice berries
6 black peppercorns
¼ level teaspoon dried sage, crumbled
2 bay leaves

1 Roll the pork cubes in the flour until coated.
Heat the oil in a flameproof casserole and cook
the pork in it, uncovered, over a moderate heat
for about 10 minutes, turning to brown all
over. Lift out the meat with a slotted spoon and
put it on kitchen paper to drain.

2 Cook the onion, carrot and garlic in the
uncovered casserole for about 5 minutes until

TIP
*This casserole
develops a richer
flavour if cooked a
day before you need
it and kept in the
refrigerator once
cooled. Before
serving, lift off
any fat from
the surface, bring
the casserole to
the boil on a
direct heat and
simmer for
10-15 minutes.*

*The sweet and sour
combination of apple,
vinegar and spices not
only makes a perfect
sauce for the lean pork,
but also helps to
tenderise the meat and
keep the warm ruby
colour of the cabbage.*

lightly coloured. Mix in the apple and cabbage, cover and cook for about 15 minutes. Stir in the vinegar, stock, allspice, peppercorns, sage, pork cubes and bay leaves. Cover the casserole and cook in the heated oven for 1 hour.

Take out the bay leaves before serving, but you can add a garnish of fresh bay leaves for a touch of rich green. Serve mashed potatoes and french beans with the casserole and offer a little pot of English mustard.

Spicy pork loin

SERVES 4
PREPARATION TIME: 5 minutes, plus 1 hour to marinate
COOKING TIME: 10 minutes

2 dried bay leaves, finely ground
1 level teaspoon ground cumin
½ level teaspoon each ground coriander and ginger
¼ level teaspoon ground turmeric
1lb (450g) boneless pork loin with fat removed, cut into 8 thin slices
Lime wedges and coriander leaves to garnish

1 Mix the ground bay, cumin, coriander, ginger and turmeric and rub into both sides of the pork slices. Cover and leave to marinate at room temperature for 1 hour.

2 Lay the pork on the grill rack and cook under a hot grill for about 10 minutes, turning 3 or 4 times, until cooked through and golden brown. Garnish with the lime and coriander.

Braised fennel or celery hearts and fresh noodles go well with this aromatic dish.

ONE SERVING
CALORIES 145
TOTAL FAT 4g
SATURATED FAT 2g
CARBOHYDRATES 0
ADDED SUGAR 0
FIBRE 0
SODIUM 85mg

TIP
Grind the bay leaves thoroughly in a mortar with a pestle, or in an electric coffee grinder. Fragments of bay are very sharp; they can stick in the throat and cause choking.

The dry Indian-style marinade creates a mouthwatering aroma whose promise is amply fulfilled in the eating.

Pork and vegetable stir-fry

SERVES 4
PREPARATION TIME: 15 minutes
COOKING TIME: 10 minutes

ONE SERVING
....
CALORIES 195
....
TOTAL FAT 7g
....
SATURATED FAT 1g
....
CARBOHYDRATES 7g
....
ADDED SUGAR 0
....
FIBRE 1g
....
SODIUM 75mg
....

Mild rice vinegar, soy sauce and amber Chinese sesame oil, together with crunchy fresh bean sprouts, add to the authenticity of this quickly made dish of crisp vegetables and tender strips of pork.

1 level tablespoon cornflour
4fl oz (115ml) chicken stock
½ teaspoon soy sauce
1 teaspoon rice vinegar or white wine vinegar
1 tablespoon sesame oil
4 tablespoons dry sherry
1 level teaspoon peeled and grated root ginger
1 clove garlic, peeled and chopped
1 medium carrot, peeled and sliced
½ red pepper, de-seeded and chopped
½ medium cucumber, peeled and sliced
4oz (115g) fresh bean sprouts, rinsed and drained
1 spring onion, trimmed and sliced
12oz (340g) pork tenderloin with fat removed, thinly sliced and cut into strips

1 Mix the cornflour to a smooth paste with 2 tablespoons of the stock. Stir in the rest of the stock, the soy sauce, the vinegar, half the oil and half the sherry.

2 Heat the remaining oil in a nonstick frying pan and toss the ginger and garlic in it over a high heat for 30 seconds. Mix in the carrot and red pepper and cook for 2 minutes, stirring.

3 Add the cucumber and cook for 1 minute, then the bean sprouts, onion and remaining sherry and cook for 1 minute more, stirring. Spoon the vegetables onto a plate and set aside.

4 Toss the pork in the pan over a high heat for about 4 minutes, until the meat starts to lose its pinkness. Return the vegetables to the pan, add the stock mixture and cook for about 1 minute, stirring, until the sauce thickens.

Serve the stir-fry piping hot with white rice to give a final Oriental touch. You can slice and fan out the cucumber tip as a garnish.

Black-eyed beans are also known as southern peas in the United States, where cooks in the south often use them to absorb bacon's flavour.

Southern bacon and beans

ONE SERVING

CALORIES 365

TOTAL FAT 10g

SATURATED FAT 3g

CARBOHYDRATES 37g

ADDED SUGAR 0

FIBRE 4g

SODIUM 950mg

SERVES 4
PREPARATION TIME: 10 minutes
COOKING TIME: 30 minutes

1 teaspoon olive oil
12oz (340g) unsmoked bacon chops or back
rashers, rind and fat removed, cut into small pieces
2 large leeks, sliced and washed
2oz (60g) chestnut mushrooms, wiped and sliced
1 level teaspoon dried marjoram
3oz (85g) long-grain rice
12oz (340g) cooked black-eyed beans
½ pint (285ml) chicken or vegetable
stock
Freshly ground black pepper

1 Heat the oil in a large, heavy-based saucepan and cook the bacon in it for 2-3 minutes. Mix in the leeks and mushrooms and cook for 5 minutes, stirring from time to time.

2 Sprinkle on the marjoram and stir in the rice for 1 minute. Mix in the cooked beans, then pour in the stock and season with pepper. Cover and simmer for about 20 minutes, or until the rice is cooked. Fluff up with a fork from time to time and pour in a little water if the mixture becomes too dry.

Garnish this hearty dish with crisp lettuce leaves and serve with a colourful tomato salad.

Gammon and lentil loaf

SERVES 8
PREPARATION TIME: 30 minutes
COOKING TIME: 1 hour 15 minutes
OVEN: Preheat to 190°C (375°F, gas mark 5)

ONE SERVING	
CALORIES 285	
TOTAL FAT 12g	
SATURATED FAT 5g	
CARBOHYDRATES 16g	
ADDED SUGAR 0	
FIBRE 2g	
SODIUM 790mg	

6oz (175g) red lentils, washed and drained
1 pint (570ml) vegetable stock
1 tablespoon olive oil
1 medium onion, peeled and chopped
2oz (60g) mushrooms, wiped and finely chopped
2 level tablespoons chopped fresh parsley
2oz (60g) wholemeal breadcrumbs
4oz (115g) Red Leicester cheese, finely grated

1lb (450g) unsmoked raw gammon, trimmed
of fat and minced
2 eggs, size 2, lightly beaten
Freshly ground black pepper

1 Bring the lentils and stock to the boil in a
large, uncovered saucepan. Lower the heat,
cover the pan and simmer for 25 minutes, or
until the lentils are soft. Drain and set aside.

2 Heat the oil in a frying pan and cook the
onion in it over a moderate heat for 3 minutes
to soften. Stir in the mushrooms and cook for a
further 2 minutes, shaking from time to time.

3 Mix the onion and mushrooms into the
lentils, work in the parsley, breadcrumbs,
cheese, gammon and eggs, and season the
mixture with pepper.

4 Line a loaf tin about 5×9in (12×23cm)
with nonstick baking paper. Spoon the
gammon mixture into the tin and level the top.
Bake in the heated oven for 1 hour 15 minutes,
until firm to the touch.   .

5 Leave to cool slightly before turning out
onto a serving plate and removing the paper.
Cut into thick slices to serve.

Serve a leafy green salad with cherry tomatoes
and parsley as colourful accompaniments. Cold
slices of the loaf, with cucumber and chutney,
are very good on open sandwiches.

*This well-flavoured meatloaf is easy to make and
can be enjoyed with jacket potatoes for a substantial
meal, or with salads for a lighter lunch.*

Gammon in plum sauce

ONE SERVING	
CALORIES 265	
TOTAL FAT 6g	
SATURATED FAT 3g	
CARBOHYDRATES 18g	
ADDED SUGAR 4g	
FIBRE 2g	
SODIUM 1280mg	

SERVES 4
PREPARATION TIME: 10 minutes
COOKING TIME: 20 minutes

1lb (450g) red dessert plums, halved and stoned
¼ pint (150ml) fresh orange juice
4 unsmoked gammon steaks, about ¼ in (6mm)
thick, each about 3oz (85g)

1 level tablespoon soft brown sugar or
demerara sugar
2 tablespoons raspberry vinegar
1 level teaspoon made English mustard
¼ level teaspoon ground cinnamon
¼ level teaspoon ground ginger
Freshly ground black pepper
Fresh dill fronds to garnish

1 Simmer the plums in the orange juice in a covered saucepan for 5-10 minutes, until the plums are soft but retain their shape.

2 Using a slotted spoon, lift 8 plum halves onto a plate and set them aside. Continue cooking the remaining plums until they are very soft. Let them cool slightly, then pour the plums and juice into a food processor and blend to a smooth purée.

3 Meanwhile, arrange the gammon steaks on the grill rack and cook them under a high heat for 6-8 minutes, turning two or three times.

4 When the gammon is almost cooked, pour the plum purée into a saucepan with the sugar and raspberry vinegar. Stir in the mustard, cinnamon and ginger, and season with pepper. Heat gently for 1-2 minutes, stirring. Put the reserved plum halves gently into the sauce and heat through for 1 minute.

5 Serve the gammon steaks garnished with the reserved plum halves, a little of the sauce and the dill fronds. Hand round the rest of the sauce separately.

Leave the diners to trim off any fat from the gammon. Cauliflower and new potatoes steamed in their skins make a pleasing contrast to the full flavours of the gammon and sauce. You can make the sauce with fresh apricots when plums are not available.

> **TIP**
> To keep the gammon steaks flat during grilling, snip them first with kitchen scissors at ½in (13mm) intervals all round the edge.

A sharp and rosy plum sauce made with fresh fruit purée is a delicious partner for mild, pink gammon steaks.

Osso bucco

ONE SERVING

CALORIES 240

TOTAL FAT 11g

SATURATED FAT 2g

CARBOHYDRATES 5g

ADDED SUGAR 0

FIBRE 1g

SODIUM 140mg

TIP
Make sure the veal is cut into four before you take it home. The butcher has the tools for sawing through the leg bone.

SERVES 4
PREPARATION TIME: 25 minutes
COOKING TIME: 2 hours

2 tablespoons olive oil
2lb (900g) veal shin or knuckle, cut into 4 rounds
1 onion, peeled and chopped
1 carrot, peeled and chopped
1 stick celery, trimmed and chopped
3 cloves garlic, peeled and finely chopped
6fl oz (175ml) dry white wine
1 large tomato, skinned, de-seeded and chopped
½ level teaspoon each dried thyme and dried sage
Freshly ground black pepper
1 bay leaf
¼ pint (150ml) beef or veal stock
2 level tablespoons chopped fresh parsley
1½ level teaspoons finely grated lemon rind
Sprigs of fresh bay or thyme to garnish

1 Heat 1 tablespoon of the oil in a large flameproof casserole and brown the veal in it over a high heat for 2 minutes on each side. Lift the veal onto a plate and set aside.

2 Reduce the heat, add the remaining oil to the casserole and cook the onion, carrot, celery and half the garlic in it for about 5 minutes, or until the onion is lightly coloured. Return the veal to the casserole, pour in the wine and cook over a moderate heat until the liquid is reduced by half.

3 Stir in the tomato, thyme and sage, season with pepper, put in the bay leaf and pour on the stock. Cover the casserole and simmer for 2 hours, or until the meat is almost falling off the bone. Pour in a little boiling water during cooking if the liquid evaporates too much.

4 Mix the parsley, lemon rind and remaining garlic. Discard the bay leaf, then sprinkle the mixture over the veal and garnish with the bay or thyme.

Serve the osso bucco with risotto rice, creamy in texture and perhaps tinted a pale gold with a few threads of saffron. A green salad makes a crisp, refreshing contrast.

The marrowbone in the veal makes a full-flavoured and slightly gelatinous broth for the meltingly tender meat in this hearty family dish.